BROADCAST DESIGN

daab

Bearing in mind the undeniable prominence of the theme of broadcast design and television branding, it seems strange that very little has been published on the matter. The colossal speed at which the industry moves seems to leave little time for contemplation and reflection, which is a shame, as this is a fascinating area of audiovisual design, both in terms of content and technology, and has many interesting phenomena worth studying and applying in other contexts.

This book is not an educational textbook, nor does it pretend to be a comprehensive guide. What it does try to do is depict and discuss very different design positions, strategic thinking and market-specific contexts in the field, using ten channels selected as examples. The main focus is of course the representation of these design positions on-air (that is, in the form of a TV signal). However, it shouldn't be forgotten that a channel's corporate design has to be transferable to other media channels – media convergence has become a feature of daily life for the field.

The people behind the design are the channels' creatives, and frequently the agencies they work for. This book seeks to make this context transparent, not only because daily business often leaves little time for developing new design concepts, but also because the collaboration between channel and agency is inspirational, enabling new ways of seeing things to emerge. Design companies often feature in the interviews alongside a channel's representatives, or elected to answer the questions themselves, in agreement with the channels' creative departments.

A further important point was to show the design of audiovisual media in their natural environment – on screen. To this end, each network represented in this book has put together a short showreel of their on-screen presentations, which you can view on the DVD available free with this book (in NTSC format).

Great changes are facing the TV landscape, in light of new distribution channels and changed content models. You could call it a paradigm shift. The next few years are sure to put the established model of a channel to the test, and creating a unique position in the ever-more bewildering marketplace looks set to become one of the deciding success factors for future competition. Keeping up with this process will entail changes for the role of design, as well as that of strategic brand development. Fuelled by the strength of its interdisciplinary nature, design is set to contribute to the transformation of what is still our number one medium.

I would like to thank all the channels, agencies and individuals who were involved in this process – without the personal involvement of many industry professionals, this book would not have been possible. And with the constant threat of deadlines looming, this collaboration cannot be praised highly enough!

Criticisms or other inspired comments are of course welcome and can best be expressed at new@bmpltd.de.

I hope you find the book enjoyable and interesting!
Björn Bartholdy, Editor

arte

France / Germany **ARTE**

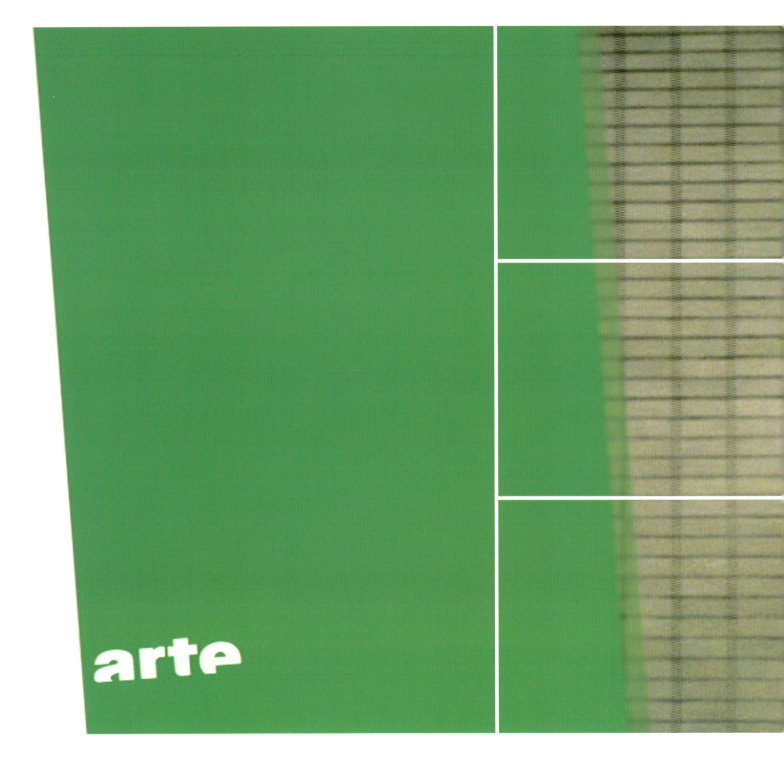

ARTE's look is based on the concept of the angle (opposite page) – plurality and use of colour embody the culture channel's content and social remit. This page: "Zoom Europa" opener.

ARTE is a strong brand with a high public profile and excellent image. With its focus on the Future and Europe it will continue to stand out from other channels and make an important contribution to legitimizing licence fee financed broadcasting. Its exceptional creativity and the high quality of its programmes are the foundation for ARTE's success and uniqueness – now and in the future.

ARTE is a European public-service cultural television channel. Its originality lays in the fact that it targets audiences from different cultural backgrounds, in particular French and German. It is composed of three entities: the headquarters in Strasbourg and two Members responsible for programme production and delivery, which are ARTE France in Paris and ARTE Deutschland TV GmbH in Baden-Baden.

ARTE France and ARTE Deutschland TV GmbH currently provide three-quarters of ARTE's programming in equal proportions, the remainder being provided by ARTE G.E.I.E. and broadcasters cooperating with ARTE. The Members are responsible for submitting programme proposals, which have to be approved by the Programme Committee and are subsequently broadcast by the headquarters. They jointly finance and control headquarters operations in Strasbourg while representing their own interests before ARTE G.E.I.E.'s advisory and decision-making bodies.

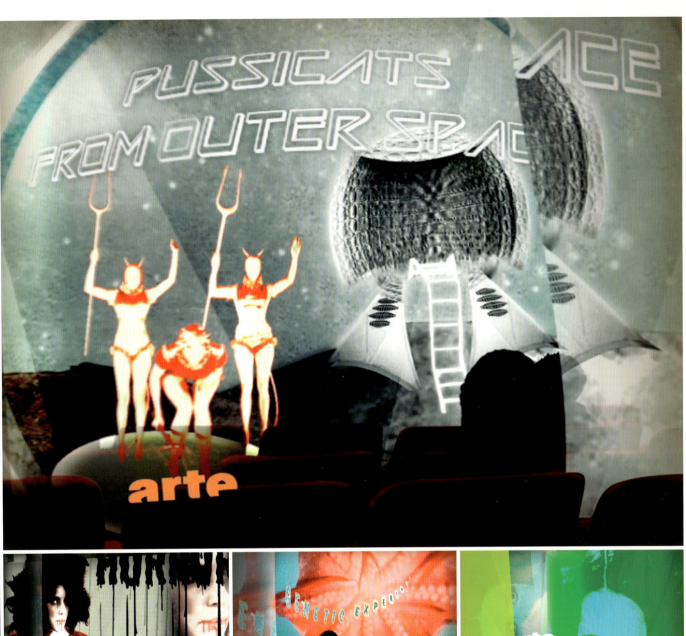

Velvet's design juxtaposes perfect images and rougher, moving ones. Both pages: "Trash" opener.

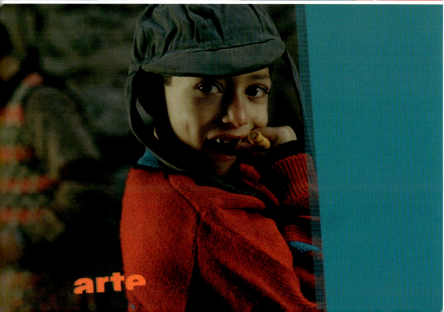

The Head of On-Air Department ARTE, Henri L'Hostis, kindly answered some questions about BROADCAST DESIGN (BD).

BD: ARTE is a German-French co-project. What unique feature does that entail for design and branding?
ARTE: Because it's aimed at a bi-national audience, ARTE cannot emphasise any exclusively national characteristics, so as not to alienate the other audience. But that's not a handicap, quite the contrary: constant incentives to stimulate creativity and originality.

BD: ARTE is a culture channel – that means challenging content for an "easily defined" target audience. Does that create certain possibilities...?
ARTE: The quality of ARTE's programming has to be reflected in the channel's design – after all, you don't wrap up Chanel perfume in an Aldi bag. So ARTE has to develop a design that has the same level of quality as the programming – without coming across as elitist. Our channel design tries to reflect the high expectations of our core audience. At the same time, we also want to seduce the kind of viewer who only tunes in to ARTE occasionally. Put simply: our design has to be original, accessible and familiar.

BD: ...Or does it create specific limitations?
ARTE: Limits? We avoid any mono-national cultural or aesthetic references, in order not to exclude German or French or European audiences.

ARTE reflects its intercultural remit! The fact that both
France and Germany have been shaped by people from many different backgrounds helps!
Pages 14-17: different ARTE brand idents.

BD: ARTE is a bilingual channel – what challenges do that bring?

ARTE: It is certainly the case that being bilingual involves a major challenge: making sure the on-screen information is readable. And there are some basic ground rules for that, e.g.: The typography for each language has a fixed colour. Systematic graphic positioning of the languages in relation to each other.

Despite this, audience research has found that viewers don't see the bilingual graphics as offering additional information, and more as something that makes them harder to read. And that's why we're now working on developing monolingual programme trailers.

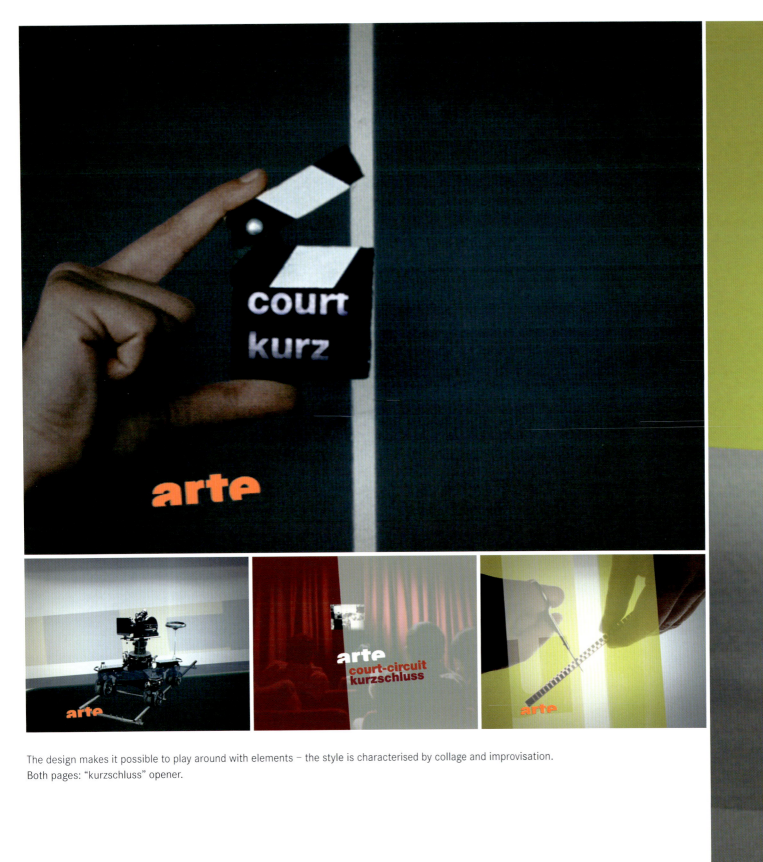

The design makes it possible to play around with elements – the style is characterised by collage and improvisation.
Both pages: "kurzschluss" opener.

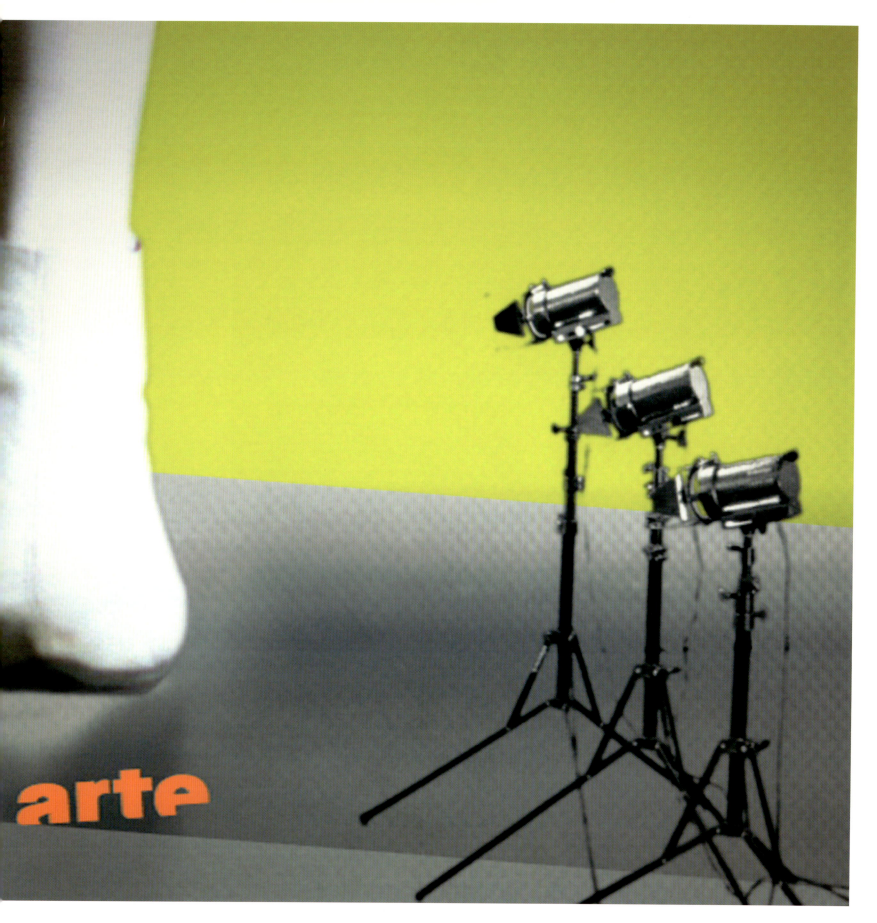

arte

BD: Can you give us an idea of the decision-making process for design? Particularly in the light of two national identities, which both have certain attitudes towards design, certain characteristics...? How do you reach a consensus?

ARTE: We start by asking ourselves the basic questions. Who are we? What are our values? Which viewers do we want to reach? Who are our competitors: In Germany? In France? In Europe? Without these definitions and positioning, any aesthetic development of our brand can only be a matter of coincidence. The core of ARTE's philosophy is defined as follows: Definition: ARTE is a culture channel aimed at European audiences.

Values: Openness; respect; (interpersonal) warmth.

Aim: To gear itself towards the curious, interested viewer.

These determiners create a kind of "backbone" for our visual presence.

A consensus can only be reached if suggestions are based on these basic determiners. Of course, aesthetic suggestions always involve an irrational element, limited by our own individual development and the respective national identity. But this shows how important it is not to let emotional creativity be your only guide. Our channel's stated basic position serves to keep us on the path. ARTE's channel design isn't art for art's sake, but always has marketing results in mind.

Both pages: "Zoom Europa" opener.

BD: What is the significance of the ARTE angle?

ARTE: The angle represents ARTE's intention to look at the world from a different perspective (than other channels). Looking at things from an unusual angle – the communications axis of ARTE is based on "curiosity".

BD: How closely does ARTE work with Velvet? Does the channel want the agency to surprise it, or do you have a symbiotic understanding that you build on?

ARTE: Using creative input from agencies is very important for us. It gives us a perspective from outside and is an effective antidote to "in-company blind spots", which develop all too easily when you're "stewing in your own juices". It's a great way for us to get feedback about our specific assets and deficits. We're always open to original and unconventional suggestions, as long as they respect our core values.

BD: Does the particular quality of ARTE's content also imply a particular attitude to design?

ARTE: The quality of the programmes reflects the quality of the design – always viewed in terms of being sufficiently accessible. Whilst the aesthetics are important, the sound is also important (how are the viewers addressed, the melody of the language, the flow...).

That's why we refuse to use any sensationalism. You can see the results of this restraint in the choice of our announcers, our sound design, our text design, and also in the fluid programme transitions and the maintaining of a certain colour harmony.

There is usually a dialogue between graphics and people – crisscrossing lines and overlays bring the two levels close together. Both pages: ARTE "kultur".

DU LUNDI AU VENDREDI
MONTAG BIS FREITAG

arte

BD: Is it possible that such an intellectual audience is immune to all attempts to make it loyal to the brand through the use of marketing?

ARTE: Creating audience loyalty to a channel is first and foremost the result of that channel's programming. The channel design has to serve the programming, and it's critical that it keeps to the following roles: a. A guide to the programmes. b. A provider of information.

The channel design plays just as significant a role in developing our own "brand". In the first case (guide to programmes and information provider), the channel design plays the "service" card. In the second case (strengthening the brand) it's playing the "audience loyalty" card. It's extremely important that these two functions complement and complete each other.

All the work has a two-fold aim: Regular viewers have to feel comfortable and at home and new viewers have to be won over.

Finding the right balance between these two poles of interest is often a question of instinct. We have to bring together the need to keep what's old and familiar, and the need to be inventive. If we succeed in this, the viewer will accept the channel's marketing and follow it with interest.

Whether for art, culture, history or technology – the visuals for the reportage segments always foreground people.
Both pages: generic opener for ARTE "reportage".

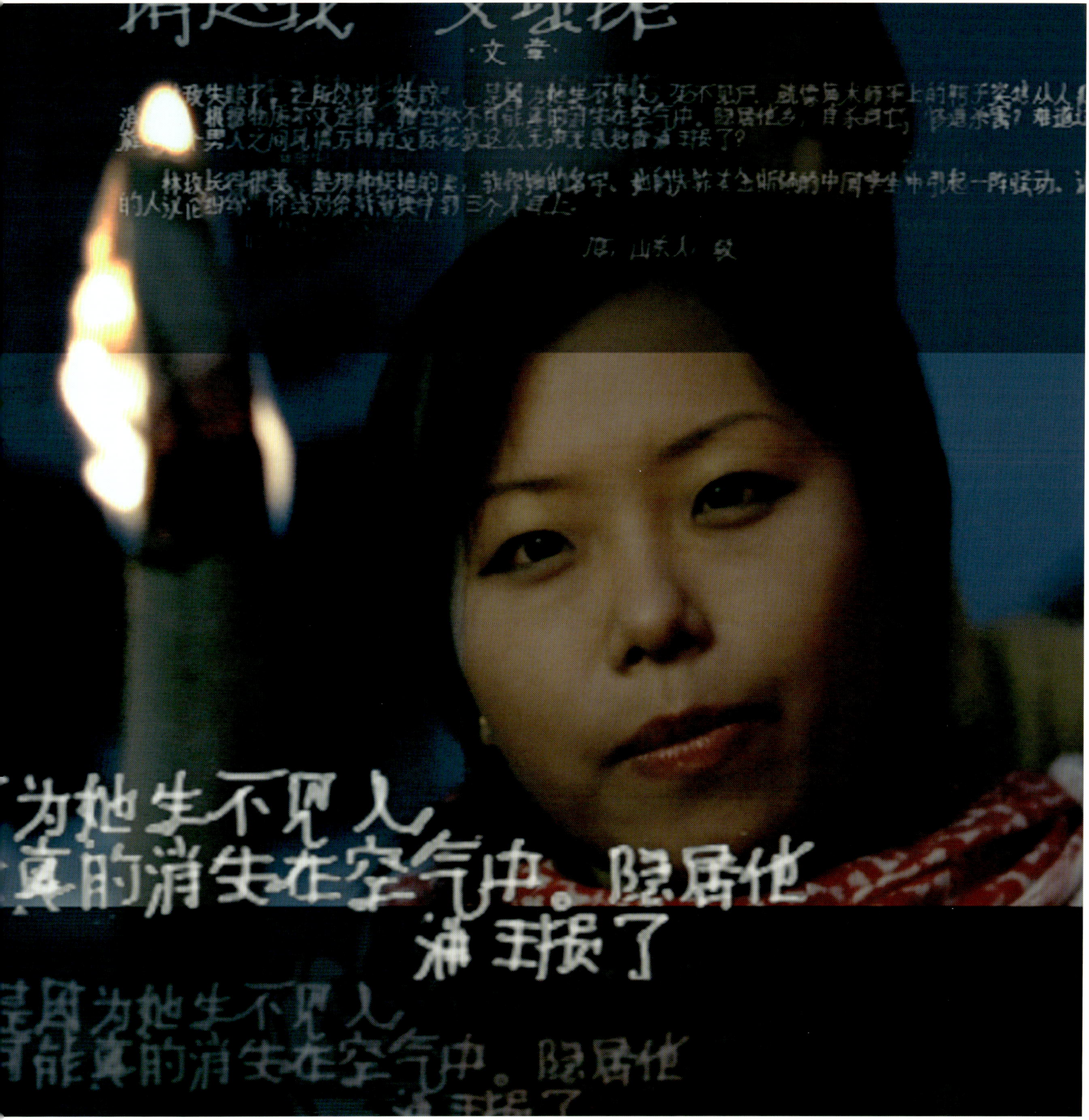

BD: How much does ARTE know about how viewers perceive the design?

ARTE: Audience research revealed two important points for us: a. ARTE profits from its strong image. The originality of its channel design is seen as a further plus point, underlining the image of a modern, original channel.

b. At the same time, a great deal of importance is attached to the functionality of the channel design: To "guide" viewers, we use a channel design that isn't always known or familiar to them, and it's extremely important that it functions.

BD: How will ARTE's design develop in the future?

ARTE: We are always keen to develop our design further, using a foundation of components that can't per se be harmoniously connected with each other: a. Promoting our own brand, b. Coming up with innovative concepts.

New concepts will have to be found to meet this challenge, which will then play out on a new field – the internet. Apart from that, integrating interactive elements is becoming more and more important – and that's an area where everything is yet to be found and invented.

6 MA
6. MÄ
GOOD B
LENI

arte

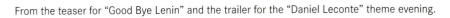

From the teaser for "Good Bye Lenin" and the trailer for the "Daniel Leconte" theme evening.

ARTE's theme evenings are an important part of the programming. Over one evening,
several programmes look at a single aspect of the world. The packaging for the theme evenings
is developed according to the respective themes.

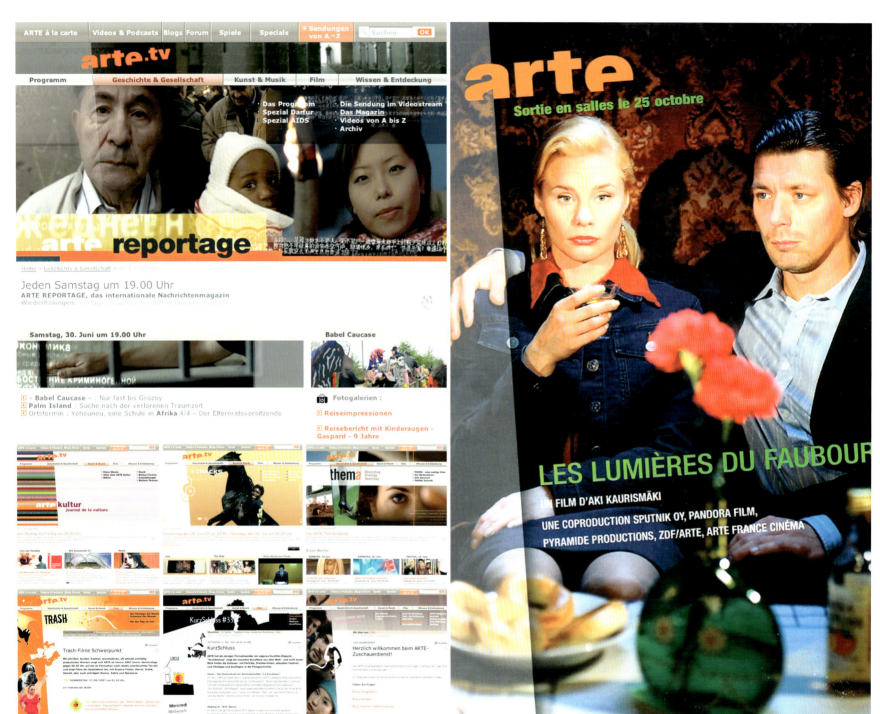

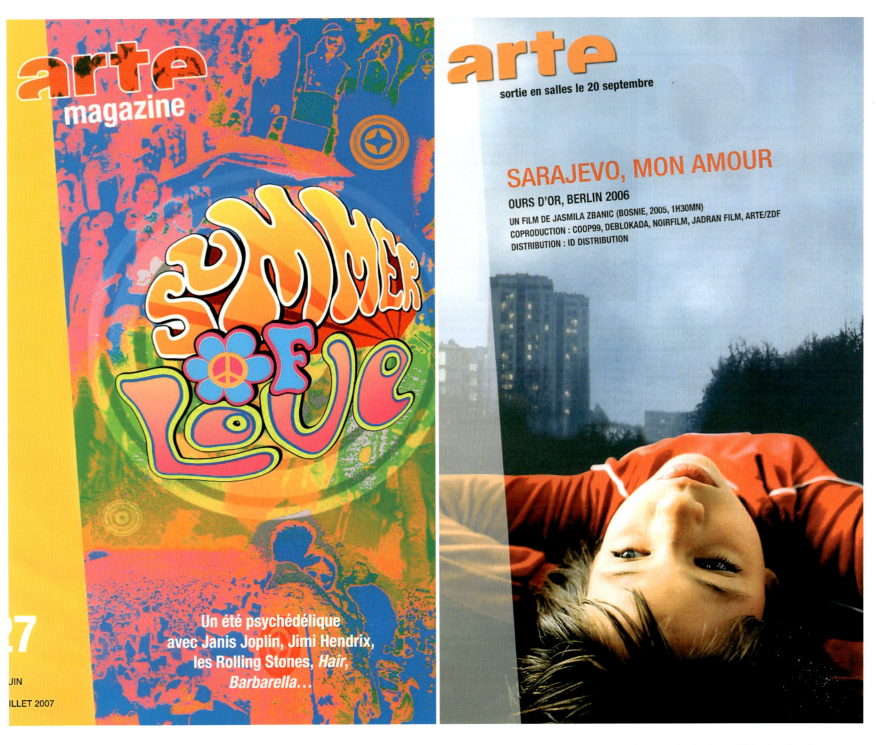

As well as a comprehensive website, ARTE's print magazine is also published twelve times a year.
Like all the channel's content, both these communication channels are available in German and French.

VELVET MEDIENDESIGN GMBH

ADRESS   Residenzstr. 7
80333 Munich, Germany

PHONE   + 49 89 36 19 47 0
FAX   + 49 89 36 19 47 19

CONTACT   contact@velvet.de
www.velvet.de

VELVET is divided into a Design Studio and Film Production Company. Flexibility is essential to our philosophy in order to adapt to the specific needs, requirements, target audiences and strategic objectives of each client. We create tailor-made design & produce challenging commercials / movies accommodating it in means of production, usability and costs.

Matthias Zentner, Designer / Director and Andrea Bednarz, Creative Director founded velvet in 1995 in Munich, Germany. They established velvet in order to be able to further their complementary experience, shared passion for design and quality and constant search for varied creative stimulus.

Rather than a company face and name, we see ourselves as a group of individuals each contributing his / her know-how and experience, interacting and united in a clear company mission, obsession, passion, a sense of humour, aesthetic values and technology research.

In terms of methodology we work within adaptable and highly-skilled creative teams which cover all the stages from concept making to fully-fledged design. Each project changes the team constellation, redefining the use of designers, concept makers, creative directors, animators, 3D-specialists, operators, directors, producers, editors, copywriters, musicians and software developers.

This teamwork allows us to keep a tight control on the creative process in all its phases and it guarantees the quality of the design we strive for. Our goal is to find all-encompassing design solutions in order to implement the Corporate Design. We cross-link concept and storyboard layout, directing and production, editing and post. Our technical equipment allows us complete in-house processing and meets our needs in top quality and controlled workflow.

Apart from direct personal contact with the client / agency, we also work actively through the Internet and our own ftp-server to overcome the time differences and distances that sometimes exist.

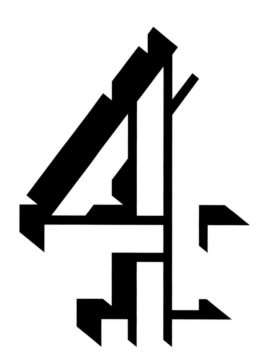

United Kingdom **CHANNEL 4**

46

Thanks to the opticals (this page), CHANNEL 4's promotion (previous page) assumes a playful character and the use of blurred wipes creates an investigative character.

The CHANNEL 4 Corporation is a publicly owned, not for profit broadcaster operating in the UK. The main public service channel, CHANNEL 4, is a free to air service funded entirely by advertising and sponsorship. Unlike the BBC it does not receive a share of the licence fee. The channel's primary purpose is the fulfilment of its public service remit, which was most recently defined in the 2003 Communications Act. This states that "the public service remit for CHANNEL 4 is the provision of a broad range of high quality and diverse programming which, in particular: a) demonstrates innovation, experiment and creativity in the form and content of programmes; b) appeals to the tastes and interests of a culturally diverse society; c) makes a significant contribution to meeting the need for the licensed public service channels to include programmes of an educational nature and other programmes of educative value; and d) exhibits a distinctive character."

As a publisher-broadcaster, CHANNEL 4 does not produce its own programmes but commissions them from more than 300 independent production companies across the UK, a far greater number than any other broadcaster, including the whole of the BBC. It works very closely with the independent production sector, and invests heavily in training and talent development throughout the industry.

The CHANNEL 4 service was originally established under the Broadcasting Act 1981 and was provided for by the Independent Broadcasting Authority. The Channel Four Television Corporation was subsequently established under the Broadcasting Act 1990 and the channel's functions were transferred over to the new Corporation in 1993. The Corporation's board is appointed by OFCOM in agreement with the Secretary of State for Culture, Media and Sport.

CHANNEL 4 transmits across the whole of the UK, except some parts of Wales, which are covered by the Welsh language S4C. It is available on all digital platforms (terrestrial, satellite and cable) as well as through traditional analogue transmission.

CHANNEL 4 also operates a number of other services, including the free-to-air digital TV channels E4 and More4, the subscription service FilmFour (which was relaunched as a free-to-air channel in summer 2006), and an ever-growing range of online activities at CHANNEL 4.com, including the broadband service FourDocs. The FilmFour production division produces and co-produces feature films for the UK and global markets.

The opticals, short animations with stencils, play with textures and details, are disorienting in the positive sense of the word, encourage the viewer to come up with interpretations.

The Creative Director of CHANNEL 4, Brett Foraker kindly answered some questions about BROADCAST DESIGN (BD).

BD: Every TV market has its own specific conditions. What are these in the UK, in terms of design and branding?
CHANNEL 4: The UK has a highly competitive TV market consisting of 5 terrestrial channels and roughly 300 cable and satellite channels. Because most are based in London, there is a high degree of design literacy across the board. It is not unusual to see some of the world's best work coming from this market. At CHANNEL 4 (and its sister channels E4, More4, and Film4) we try our best to be at the head of this field.

BD: CHANNEL 4 is pursuing a very ambitious concept in its communication strategy. How would you summarise the most important aspects of the strategy?
CHANNEL 4: CHANNEL 4's strategy has always been about creating impact with viewers. This manifests itself in three basic tenets. These might be summarised as engagement, entertainment, and navigation. Engagement starts with presenting the viewer with an arresting visual. The more iconic the image, the more you draw the viewer's attention. From there you must keep them entertained. Audiences expect this in even the shortest communication, so we're beholden as creatives to at least make the effort. Now, assuming that you have been reasonably successful in these first two tasks, you most give the viewer a clear directive. In the case of CHANNEL 4, this takes the form of a graphic language to help the viewer navigate the channel schedule. But maybe all of this sounds too pretentious? Basically, we just try to give the viewers 'treats' at every turn and trust that this will keep them tuned in and listening!

night 9.00pm

nie's

hool Dinners

nel4.com/schooldinners

Information is created through transparency; "looking behind things" is the basic design principle
(previous pages "on-air promotion", this page optical).

BD: Great Britain was and is an important motor in terms of an international language for graphics and design. Is that still the case today? Where do print, product, fashion etc. interact with audiovisual design?

CHANNEL 4: Great Britain is still one of the most vital hubs for international design. There's great stuff coming from virtually every region. London particularly has an extremely high concentration of talent and it isn't unusual to bump into several of the world's top designers on a Thursday pub crawl.

BD: CHANNEL 4 uses a lot of live action. How would you evaluate that in view of the fact that solutions, which primarily rely on graphics, are considerably more cost-effective to make and also seem to be very in at the moment?

CHANNEL 4: There is no one, singular approach. CHANNEL 4 tries to use an ever-evolving combination of live-action, hand-drawn and computer-generated techniques to create its branding and promotions. One might argue that live-action allows a greater degree of nuance and thus fares better for repeat viewing, but in general there must be a balance between all of these styles for the channel to feel well rounded.

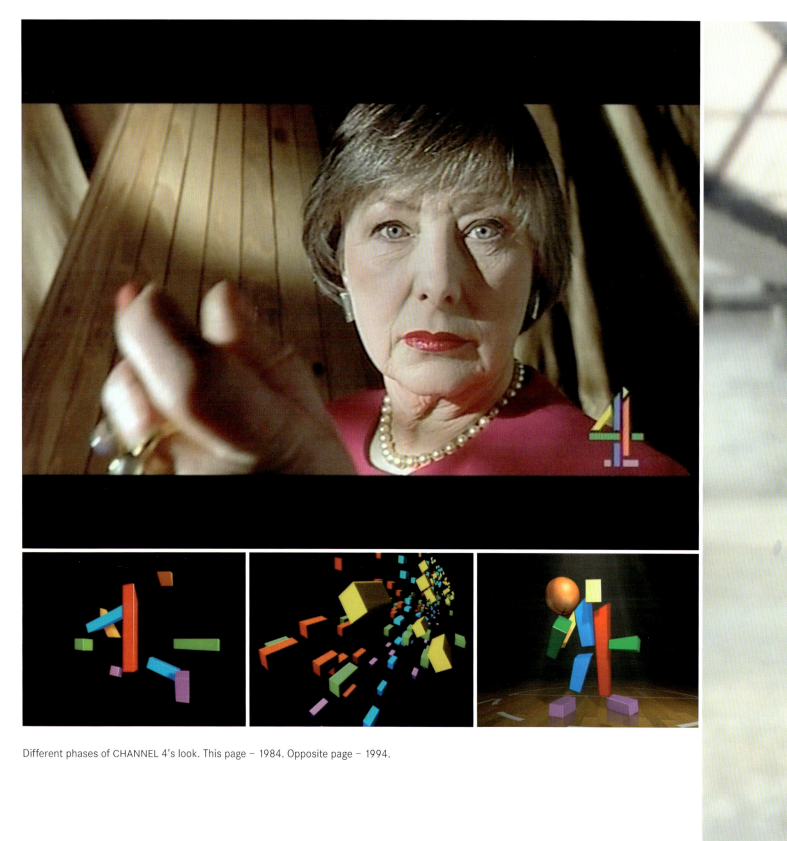

Different phases of CHANNEL 4's look. This page – 1984. Opposite page – 1994.

BD: The majority of British households now receive TV through digital distribution channels. Does that have any implications for design? From the design point of view, where do the challenges for new formats and the transformation of the medium towards an audience-driven model lie?

CHANNEL 4: The rise of digital formats is clearly very exciting. But the idea that the audience will prefer to see an unending supply of dull, homemade DV is misleading. I think the greatest opportunities lay lie not with the normal consumer, but with the undiscovered talents who lack an outlet. We have been running a scheme for the past 5 years with Creative Review to help bring some of this talent into the light. You can see this work on-air on E4 or www.channel4. com / estings. Also, our in-house agency 4Creative has a talent scout who is constantly on the look-out for cutting edge work from around the world.

BD: How is CHANNEL 4 going to respond to these new changes in viewer behaviour?

CHANNEL 4: In terms of an on-going response, CHANNEL 4 will continue to support nascent talent and to employ as diverse a group of designers as we can. Our current roster includes Rudd Studio, Spin, Pete & Tom, Dan Eatock, Grant Gilbert, Clare Price, Noah Harris, Man v. Machine and Olly Reid to name a few.

Friends

8.00am
Big Brother's
Little Brother

next
Big Brother

8.30am
Beat The
Nation

9.30am

The interplay between 2D and 3D creates its own take on depth.
The viewer is always looking into things from CHANNEL 4's perspective.

BD: Brett, you've gained quite a lot of experience in advertising over the years. Where do you see the differences between work for advertising clients and work for TV clients?

CHANNEL 4: Advertising clients and TV clients basically want the same thing: to be talked about. My job as a director is to create images that will engage the viewer and get them talking about the product in question. Whether this is a car, a mobile phone, or a TV programme, the approach doesn't change too much. The most notable difference is that the creation of ads involves several extra layers of bureaucracy that can either help or hinder a particular creative concept. In my experience, the best agencies behave in a very similar way to the best TV companies. They seek simplicity at every stage of the process. As a director these are always the best environments in which to work.

BD: How important are strategic decisions, which concern the channel's development for the evolution of CHANNEL 4's on air branding?

CHANNEL 4: Of course, overarching strategic decisions are very important to our on-going branding initiatives. On a corporate level these may refer to specific demographics that need to be targeted or specific seasons that need promotion. These are probably most evident in our various channel launches (More4, Film4, etc).

The principles of instability and transience are also carried over into the idents.
The channel's logo only comes together for the observer at one specific angle, only to break up a second later.

BD: Audiovisual design – and broadcast design in particular – show stronger tendencies towards internationalisation than almost any other field of design. What is more predominate in this process: the moment of swapping ideas, or the inspiration from a worldwide pool of ideas and creative resources?

CHANNEL 4: Given that much of advertising is incredibly derivative, we try our best to furrow new ground. Within our creative teams, the swapping and sharing of ideas is paramount. Finding 'reference material' on YouTube is no substitute for originality. Instead, everyone at C4 is encouraged to freely contribute to the work of their peers and to receive constructive advice in return. The channel identity, for example, is a direct result of the intensive collaboration between Russell Appleford, Matt Rudd – who is responsible for all the graphics – and myself. Notwithstanding the results, it is a fun and fulfilling way to work.

BD: The content positioning of a channel is not unimportant for the visual strategy... How does this work in CHANNEL 4's case?

CHANNEL 4: CHANNEL 4's content changes constantly, but its remit – which stresses creativity, innovation and challenging accepted thinking – does not. We work primarily to the remit and attempt to evolve as the needs of the channel change. This way, we can proceed organically rather than undergo a massive re-branding exercise every time somebody in a suit sneezes.

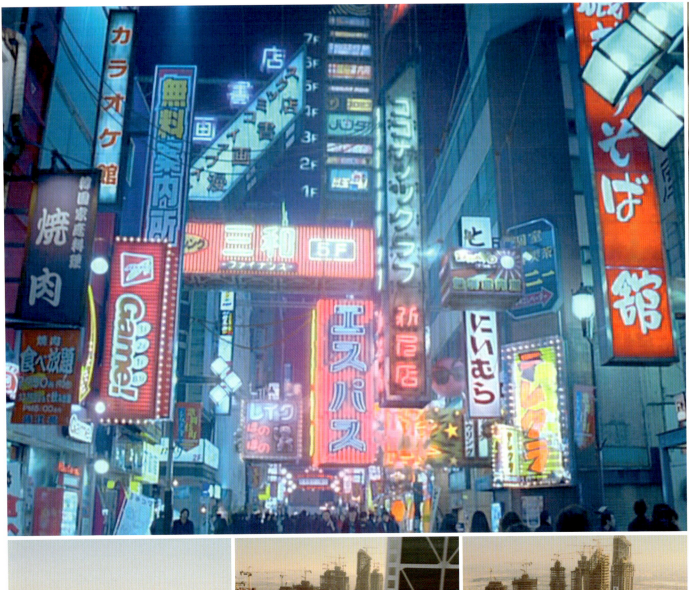

The settings for the idents range from the rich backdrop of South-East Asia to a dingy English housing estate.
You can find projection surfaces for the CHANNEL 4 brand anywhere!

BD: Is there such a thing as a "CHANNEL 4 path" in terms of carrying out projects? How does the creative process generally work?

CHANNEL 4: Sidney Lumet once said something to the effect that 'casting is 90% of film-making'. I suppose that C4's philosophy is similar when it comes to executing creative work. We like to put the very best talent together with the right project and then stay out of the way! Notwithstanding the aforementioned designers, over the past years we've worked with such talented people as Jim Fiscus, David Lachappelle, Ellen Von Unwerth, David Modell, Alistair Thain, David Levinthal, Simon Rattigan, Phil Lind, Kevin Spacey, Neil Gorringe, Rocky Morton, and Tom Tagholm among many others. If I were to summarise our creative process, I'd say this: keep the idea simple, hire the best person for the job, let them get on with it.

BD: To what extent are our images dominated by the possibilities of the tools we use? Could it be that the road back to the analogue world is the only salvation from this misery?

CHANNEL 4: Lately, I've come to think that an interesting path lies in combining very old practical techniques with contemporary 3-D animation and digital compositing. I've recently completed a project where we built a Tesla coil and then captured the results to be manipulated in Inferno as stand alone effects. These sat-in very well with both the 3-D and the live-action shots in the rest of the edit.

British celebrity chef Jamie Oliver cooks for children and young people in "Jamie's School Dinners".
Comments and graffitti appear in "real time".

Off-air, the brand also uses very few elements: Billboard in London's West End.

School Dinners
23 Feb 9.00pm

School Dinners
23 Feb 9.00pm

Imagine a world without religion

The Root Of All Evil?
Coming soon

Tsunami: Where was God?
Christmas Day 7.50pm

The British Working Class
Class in Britain series starts Sunday 10th July 8pm

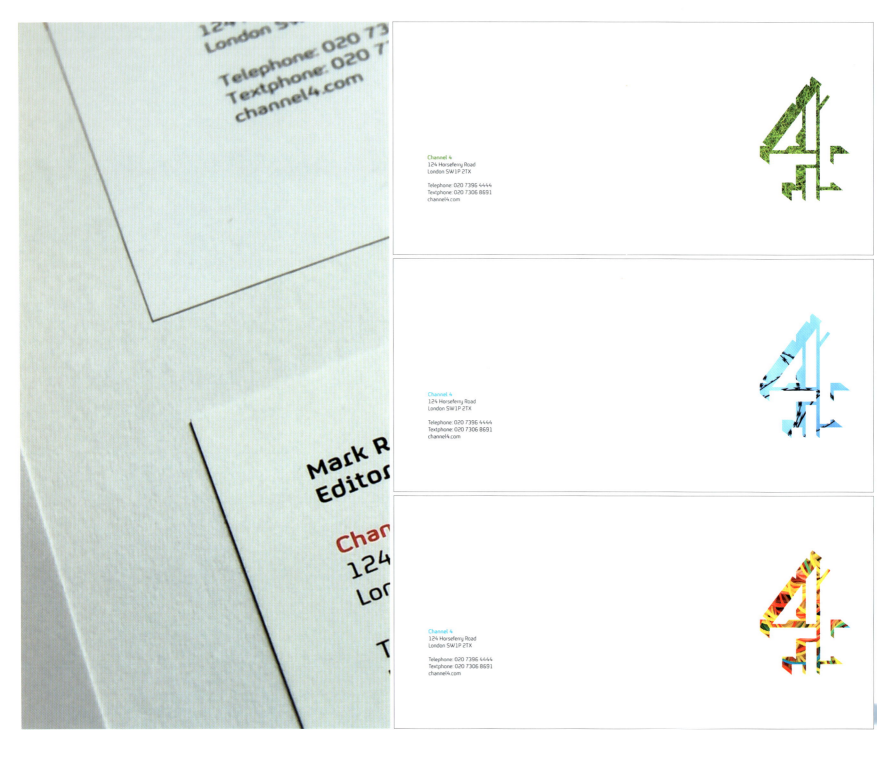

Channel 4
124 Horseferry Road
London SW1P 2TX

Telephone: 020 7396 4444
Textphone: 020 7306 8691
channel4.com

Channel 4
124 Horseferry Road
London SW1P 2TX

Telephone: 020 7396 4444
Textphone: 020 7306 8691
channel4.com

Channel 4
124 Horseferry Road
London SW1P 2TX

Telephone: 020 7396 4444
Textphone: 020 7306 8691
channel4.com

Name
Title

Channel 4
124 Horseferry Road
London SW1P 2TX

Telephone: 020 7396 4444
Direct Line: 020 7306 3777
Direct Fax: 020 7306 6945
Mobile: 07971 000 000
email@channel4.co.uk
channel4.com

Name
**Title Runs Over
Two Lines**

Channel 4
124 Horseferry Road
London SW1P 2TX

Telephone: 020 7396 4444
Direct Line: 020 7306 3777
Direct Fax: 020 7306 6945
email@channel4.co.uk
channel4.com

Name
**Title Runs Over
Two Lines**

Channel 4
124 Horseferry Road
London SW1P 2TX

Telephone: 020 7396 4444
Direct Line: 020 7306 3777
Direct Fax: 020 7306 6945
Mobile: 07971 000 000
email@channel4.co.uk
channel4.com

Name
Title

Channel 4
124 Horseferry Road
London SW1P 2TX

Telephone: 020 7396 4444
Direct Line: 020 7306 3777
Direct Fax: 020 7306 6945
email@channel4.co.uk
channel4.com

Even serious means of communication hint at the channel's multidimensional character.
Examples of CHANNEL 4's print design.

Channel 4 Typeface

Headline	Text	Condensed
C4 Headline	C4 Text Regular	C4 Condensed Regular
C4 Guide	*C4 Text Italic*	*C4 Condensed Italic*
	C4 Text Medium	**C4 Condensed Bold**
Menu	*C4 Text Medium Italic*	***C4 Condensed Bold Italic***
C4 Menu	**C4 Text Bold**	
	C4 Text Bold Italic	

Character Set C4 Headline

abcdefghijklmnopqrstuvwx
yzßæœfiflABCDEFGHIJKLM
NOPQRSTUVWXYZÆŒ&012
3456789*#@+<=>'''÷±%‰/
µ£$€ƒ¥¢,.:;..."""«»‹›·,,!?¿¡(/)[\
](|)®©ÄÅÂÁÃÀÇÉÊËÈÍÎÏÌÑØ
ÓÔÒÖÕÜÚÛÙŸáàâäãåçéèê
ëíìîïñøóòôöõúùûüÿ†‡§°ª¬•¶
1°˜^˄˜˘˙˚-‒—_

So let's go then, down the tunnel to the platform where mannequin children smile, supermodels glide, sharks loom, heads bleed, Myra Hindley stares and the trains are rushing in and the passengers are getting out and the next stop is St Thomas Aquinas, for the Comedians and Footballers Lines.

Matthew Collings, This is Modern Art

So let's go then, down the tunnel to the platform where mannequin children smile, supermodels glide, sharks loom, heads bleed, Myra Hindley stares and the trains are rushing in and the passengers are getting out and the next stop is St Thomas Aquinas, for the Comedians and Footballers Lines.

Matthew Collings, This is Modern Art

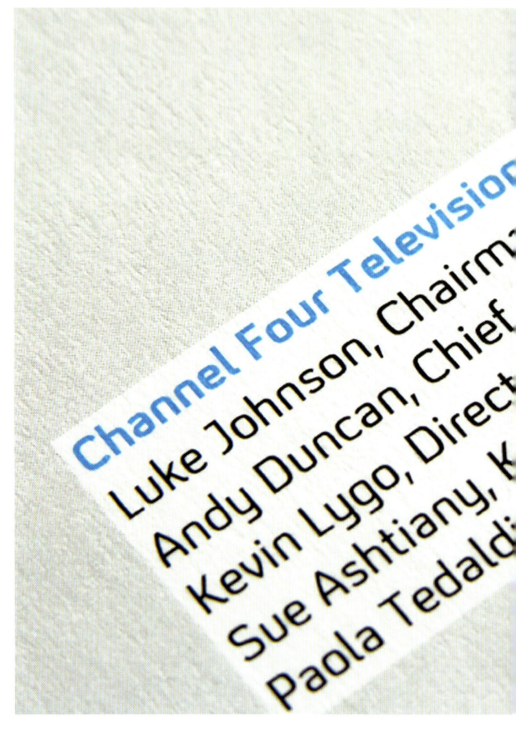

Channel Four Television
Luke Johnson, Chairm...
Andy Duncan, Chief...
Kevin Lygo, Direct...
Sue Ashtiany, K...
Paola Tedaldi...

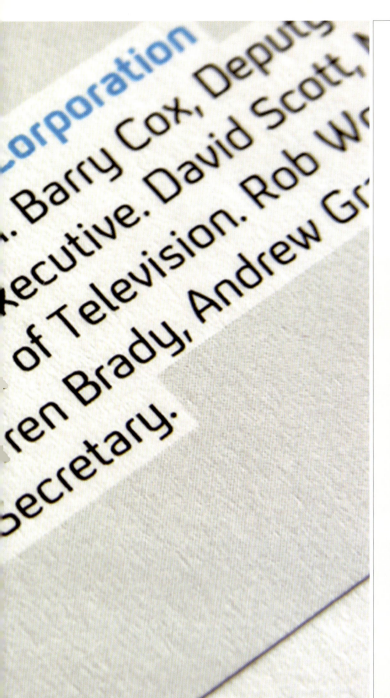

International

Channel Four International Limited
Registered in Cardiff under no. 2797368 Registered Office: 124 Horseferry Road, London SW1P 2TX, England.

The use of a font developed especially for CHANNEL 4 – by Jason Smith – guarantees a unique character, as well as clear readability across a range of media channels.

PlugTV / Belgium **PLUG**

All sorts of characters inhabit PlugTV's world. Both pages: "Elastimouth" ident series.

For all young people between 15 and 34 years of age, PlugTV is a general, different and surprising television channel, thanks to its strong, varied programming essentially comprising cult films and series, reality TV, crazy entertaining broadcasts and music programmes (concerts, music videos, etc.).

The tone is simultaneously fun, Zen, with no taboos, on the edge of provocation, trash or irreverence. The station look is hyper trendy, representative of young people of today.

PlugTV, Belguim, is part of the RTL Group. While the other TV channels, RTL and Club RTL, cover the more traditional end of the spectrum, PlugTV was created as an answer to foreign and local music / youth channels such as MTV and MCM. From the start the founding team of Olivier Pairoux and Eusebio Larrea had had a lot of freedom when making their vision reality. This resulted in a TV channel that was meant to differ from its competitors. More daring, fun, controversial, diverse and most importantly, slightly deranged.

SEVEN Productions created a set of building blocks for PlugTV's design which reflect current trends in illustration and animation. Style and surprise are the main features. Both pages: from the station ident "Les Oiseaux Heureux".

The Creative Director of SEVEN, the external communication and branding agency of PlugTV, Sven Mastbooms (> p. 118) kindly answered some questions about BROADCAST DESIGN (BD).

BD: PLUG's look is pretty loud! How come the channel is confident enough to present itself like that?

SEVEN: PlugTV is part of the RTL Group. While the other TV channels, RTL and Club RTL, cover the more traditional end of the spectrum, PlugTV was created as an answer to foreign and local music / youth channels such as MTV and MCM. From the start the founding team of Olivier Pairoux and Euse-bio Larrea had had a lot of freedom when making their vision reality. This resulted in a TV channel that was meant to differ from its competitors. More daring, fun, controversial, diverse and most importantly, slightly deranged.

The result is also due to the confidence both the marketing and on-air management at the RTL Group had in the talent of the founding team. This confidence is essential for creating outstanding and diverse work. That kind of confidence is surprising, considering that PlugTV is a commercial TV station. They are really open to external people working together in the same spirit.

The universe that was created for PlugTV is being extended to launch PLUGMOBILE, PlugTV's mobile operator. Some of the characters from the PlugTV universe have become the faces for the launch campaign. The backgrounds were shot on HDTV in Brussels. After the footage was graded, 3D characters and graphics were added to bring it all to life...

BD: Is that radical approach typically Belgian?

SEVEN: It's hard to say. As you know Belgium is divided into two language zones: Flemish-speaking Flanders in the north and French-speaking Wallonie in the south. SEVEN happens to work as a communication and branding agency for the biggest youth TV channels on both sides: JIM in the north, PlugTV in the south.

For both channels we use a certain tone of voice that results in what we call distinctive brand 'attitudes'. The feeling you have with both brands is not necessarily determined by baselines and Pantone colours but by a sort of humour and poetry that makes them stand out from the pack. So I can't say whether this radical approach is typically Belgian rather than typically SEVEN.

For JIM the tone of voice is even more in your face and burlesque. For PlugTV we added more aesthetics and poetry on top of the radical humour. We were told that apparently the south is known for playing more with words but is in general not as avant garde as the north. I think PlugTV proves that that's an understatement and it really makes a difference in that respect. As such, PlugTV is very often able to explore and widen boundaries.

BD: How do viewers respond to the channel's look and corporate image?

SEVEN: Very, well actually. One night after a PlugTV party I was in a shuttle bus on my way to the car park when I overheard other passengers in the bus talking about some of the movies we had created for the branding.

Apparently they knew quite some of the movies by heart and were discussing which movies they already knew and which they still had to discover. It was quite fun to hear other people quote 'Hubba hubba Bang Bang' from the movies in which the puppy gets slaughtered in different ways.

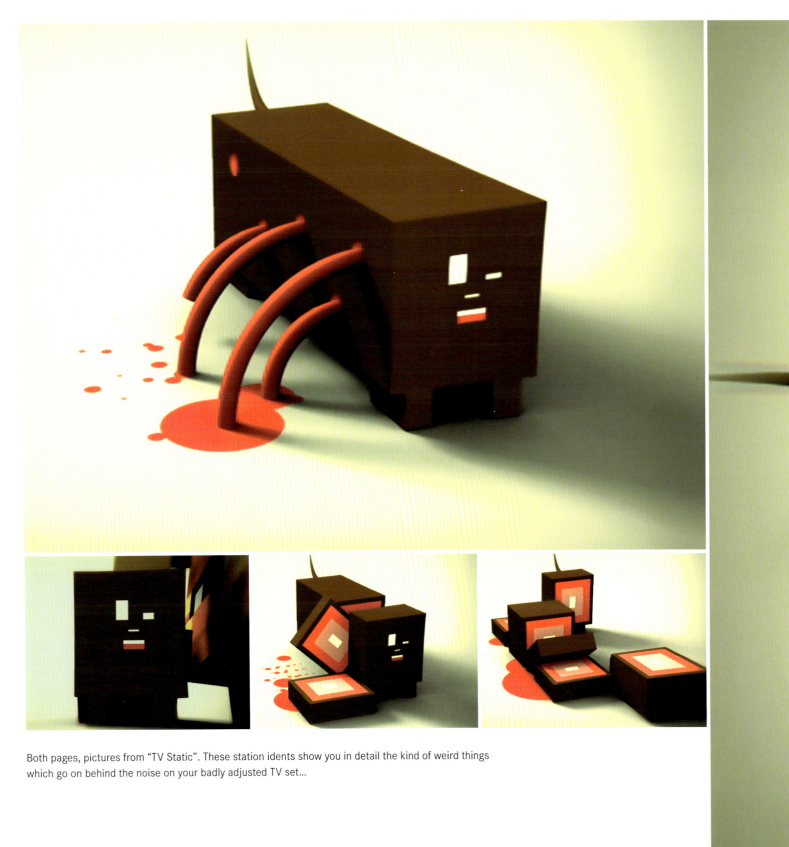

Both pages, pictures from "TV Static". These station idents show you in detail the kind of weird things which go on behind the noise on your badly adjusted TV set...

BD: Please give a brief description of the most important parameters for PLUG's design.
SEVEN: The most important parameters at the briefing: PlugTV = generic alternative channel for the audience 15-25, predominantly male profile.
Tone of voice = fun, zen, no taboos, provocative, deranged, original, aspirational, humour.

BD: Why did you decide to work with so many different characters and stories? How do you hold the brand identity together in the face of all the variety?
SEVEN: From the start PlugTV was positioned as a very diverse TV station. The branding frequently changes and evolves to emphasise that. We tried to create a general coherence by creating a PLUG Universe populated with characters that somehow reflect many different characteristics of the viewers. Therefore we developed an image campaign with characters reflecting those different characteristics. PlugTV, the TV channel of those in love, the angry, the emotional, the playful, the shy, the lazy, etc.. At the end of the commercial the viewer is invited to take a seat on the PlugTV sofa. After all, everybody has a twisted side. We adapted the same concept for the on air branding where we were able to introduce more characters and storylines. We tried to make the whole branding coherent by creating different episodes per character. The baseline 'Complètement PLUG' (Completely PLUG) stood for PlugTV as a generic youth channel with music, movies, series, reality, etc. but also for 'Completely Nuts'. It emphasised the diversity of both the channel and its viewers. That was the basic message that we tried to communicate.

CONTINUE?
Y / N

PlugTV does minimalism as well as opulence. Examples from "Work It".

J'ai cueilli de

BD: PlugTV has a very successful presence on a variety of media platforms. Did the channel's design envisage that from the start, and what are the most important parameters for that kind of flexibility?

SEVEN: PlugTV's mother company RTL has a strong strategy of exploring different media platforms. We at SEVEN like to play with opportunities in that direction as well. Some of the possibilities of the movies however haven't been explored. For example the short dialogues between the bird and the rabbit (La Pie et Lapin) were intended to be adapted for the web as well. The audience was meant to use them as e-cards, adding their own dialogues and jokes. The best of them could have then been translated back to the TV screen thanks to the simple animation concept. The short animations with the unfortunate puppy were conceived as a sort of 'game over' movie for a (mobile) game in which you had to manoeuvre your puppy between the killer pixel people.

Because of the size of the channel and its budgets, it's impossible to explore fully all the opportunities. Evidently there are more strategic and commercial multi platform opportunities at PlugTV such as Nouvelle Star (Star Academy) that successfully translated to both the internet, mobile content and even a mobile phone package with content installed on the phone. It's really in PlugTV's genes to explore content in the broadest way possible. Interaction with the audience is considered a priority. Most recently PlugTV created www.zapface.com, a social bookmarking community platform.

As a branding or communication partner one always has to keep these possibilities in mind. Sometimes concepts become bigger than life. It's really fun when that happens. After all, you can't force the audience to pick something up.

fleurs pour toi.

LES LAPINS TIMIDES

...ET VOUS

Optimistes

Voyageurs

Et vous?

Timides

Left: storyboard images and final stills from PlugTV's image campaign spot.
This page: "Les Lapins Timides" from PlugTV's image campaign.

Rebels

Motivés

LES SUPER VISÉS

LES PAS COMMANDES

LES RANCUNIERS

BD: Does the design reflect the Web 2.0 aesthetic?

SEVEN: From a design standpoint, there are not really any specific Web 2.0 elements in the design vocabulary that are used. I think the 2.0 elements are more to be found in the philosophy of the channel in general rather than in its design. There's a huge eagerness for dialogue with the audience. Initiatives like the social community site www.zapface.com and gimmicks like the Videomathon are good examples. The Videomathon is a small photo booth with a video camera in it that PlugTV takes along to parties, festivals, etc.. People are invited to create their own video messages and answers to weird questions that can later be aired or watched on the site. As an extension of the image campaign with the weird creatures in it, the audience could have their picture taken on the PlugTV sofa and have them posted online. As such they really became part of the campaign. As an outside partner we offer elements to contribute to this 'bigger picture'.

BD: The Belgian TV market is tiny. Where do your influences come from? How much interaction do you have with neighbouring countries?

SEVEN: There's little or no physical interaction with neighbouring countries, but there's always the internet making the world a much smaller place in terms of getting exposed to other people's work. As far as influences go, they are of course not limited to the aforementioned. We get inspiration from music, books, toy characters, situations from daily life and all of the other usual suspects.

BD: The first impression you get from PlugTV is that it looks like fun – how much strategy is involved?

SEVEN: PlugTV is an entertainment channel. By selecting the specific team from the launch of the channel they chose to position themselves as edgy, confrontational and slightly cuckoo. I can only support that strategy because it enables us to create the sort of work that we really love.

Designer toys and a life-sized voodoo doll suit for PlugTV's image campaign. The camouflaged teddy bear also appears in his natural habitat on the previous page.
Right: characters from PLUGMOBILE's launch spot call and text with PlugTV's own mobile operator.

BD: PlugTV's mobile content is especially interesting! Do the applications here maybe indicate a future direction for broadcast design?

SEVEN: Although every platform has its specific opportunities and limitations I don't think that makes a difference for the user / viewer. He'll want to be informed or entertained in any way he likes or can afford. We always consider the content to be priority number one. We will happily and eagerly adopt whatever medium happens to be the next big thing in broadcast design. Of course mobile content presence will expand rapidly over the next couple of years, but who knows what channel or medium we will be developing content for, say, five or ten years from here?

BD: The channel is fairly specialized, does that create particular challenges or advantages for the communication design?

SEVEN: The challenge in designing for PlugTV's audience lies in the fact that it is rather spoilt in terms of creative broadcast design. It's becoming harder and harder to create stuff that's totally new, things the audience have never seen before, because they've grown up in a very visual-oriented culture.

The exact same thing is a blessing on the other hand: because they are used to trendy and cutting-edge design, PlugTV's viewers are very open to new things, and that allowed us to be much more creative and 'in your face' than would ever be possible on any of RTL's more 'generic' channels.

BD: Where is PlugTV taking us? Will the future distribution channels play a role here?

SEVEN: Within the RTL Group, PlugTV always had a spearheading role when it comes to exploring new content, tone of voice and distribution channels.

Being the most adventurous channel of the RTL Group and also being a place for new talents and ideas to grow to fruition, PlugTV is the perfect vehicle to do so. So in short, yes!

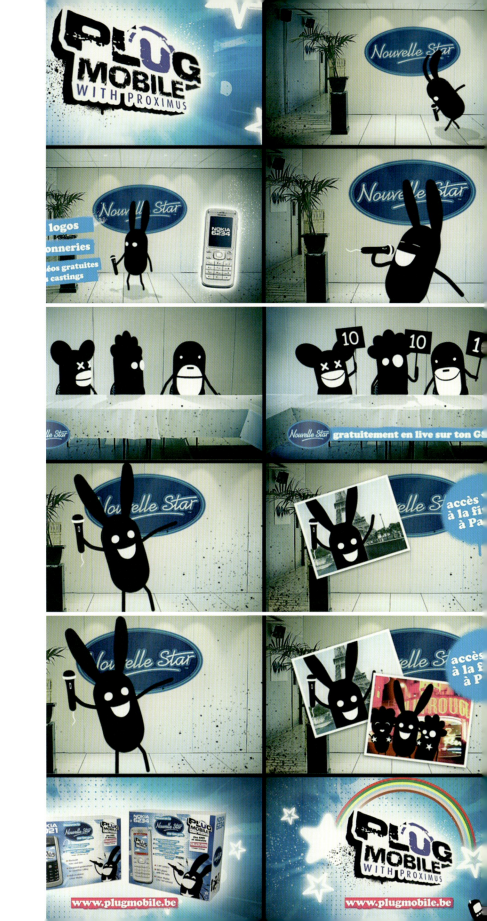

PLUGMOBILE welcome pack booklet cover – this page.
Right page: Designer toy versions of PlugTV's characters invade the SEVEN headquarters.

PlugTV has achieved total saturation of both the real and the virtual world.
Left: desktop wallpaper.
Top right: proposal for merchandising – PlugTV tape.
Bottom right: Boomerang postcards (offered for free in public spaces).

SEVEN

ADRESS

Zorgvliet 17
2860 Sint-Katelijne-Waver
Belgium

PHONE   +32 15 45 17 77
FAX   +32 15 21 74 72

CONTACT

Sven Mastbooms
sven.mastbooms@sevenproductions.be
www.sevenproductions.be

At their mansion in the mysterious forests just minutes outside Brussels (Belgium), SEVEN brews its magic potions. They mix every imaginable technique, style and medium into powerful branding and communication. For SEVEN branding is about telling stories.

Always on the look for interesting projects and interesting people to work for, SEVEN has evolved from a pure branding studio to a hybrid communication agency.

'We're not an 'ivory tower agency', says Creative Director Sven Mastbooms, 'We love to work together with our clients to create a bigger story.'

SEVEN's biggest asset is the combination of strategy, concept, design and production, and their experience in translating the 'big idea' into through the line communication. Because that's where it all starts: with good, innovative ideas.

The journey being as important as the destination, SEVEN's principles are reflected not only in their on air, print and online work but also in the design of their own studio. From dungeon to attic, the people at SEVEN have designed a very personal and inspirational atmosphere to work in.

SEVEN has won several awards at Promax / BDA and Eyes & Ears. In 2006 they received the Eyes & Ears special prize, 'Innovation' for the PlugTV on-air branding and communication.

The in house team, 12 strong, is often enlarged with freelance directors, animators, writers and designers. They have worked as a branding and communication agency for TV stations, movie distributors, food and beverage, banks and telecom clients such as JIM TV, PlugTV, 20th Century Fox Belgium / the Netherlands, Fortis, Mine, Stella Artois, Jupiler, Studio 100, Philips and the National Lottery.

ProSieben / Germany **PROSIEBEN**

ProSieben's stars on a secret mission: the channel's STAR FORCE campaign broke new ground for German TV!

Germany's Best-Known Claim! ProSieben is German television's hottest, most profiled and most popular brand. It is characterised by being a market leader and innovator in many areas (e.g. design, image, film offers). If they could only receive one channel, the vast majority of 14 to 49 year olds in Germany would choose ProSieben, according to a recent forsa poll. Furthermore, the channel's slogan "WE LOVE TO ENTERTAIN YOU" is the most widely recognised slogan of any TV channel in Germany: eighty per cent of 14-49 year olds and a massive eighty nine per cent of 14 to 29 year olds recognise it!

Must-See TV for the young media generation! With the "best films", ProSieben has long been recognised as a leading channel – and 2007 saw this image further strengthened. Its blockbusters help make ProSieben number one in Germany and according to a recent forsa poll, the channel also shows the "best entertainment", the "best evening drama series" – particularly the "best mysteries", the "best American and British comedies" and the "best medical dramas" – and also has the "best afternoon programmes" and the "best science / factual shows" on German TV! As a channel for the young and young at heart – the core audience is among 14 to 29 year olds – ProSieben is confident, cheeky, young, sexy, high quality, desirable and a trend setter. The mission is: ProSieben is must-see TV for the young media generation. The message: WE LOVE TO ENTERTAIN YOU!

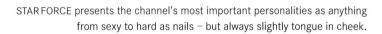

STAR FORCE presents the channel's most important personalities as anything from sexy to hard as nails – but always slightly tongue in cheek.

The Director Creative Solutions of ProSiebenSAT.1 Production, Markan Karajica, and the Director Marketing of ProSieben, Malte Hildebrandt, kindly answered some questions about BROADCAST DESIGN (BD).

BD: A plural TV market like the German one is extremely competitive. How do you create a unique channel brand in that kind of environment?
PROSIEBEN: By working to create a brand that has a clear position for the audience and by a sustained and consistent manifestation of that positioning across all channels and other media. Building up and meeting expectations is just as important a part of that as the carefully guided use of faces, colours, shapes, sounds, voices.

BD: A lot of ProSieben's work uses personalities from the channel. Was that a branding and design concept, or do approaches like that come more from the programming?
PROSIEBEN: The brand and its image campaign are in constant dialogue with the channel's content, its programmes. The faces, which represent the channel brand, originate from the format content. In this way, the image campaign backs up the programming, it's not just a pointless end in itself. The concept of the brand / design campaign exaggerates and glorifies the faces in a positive way, thus increasing the familiarity and popularity of the characters.

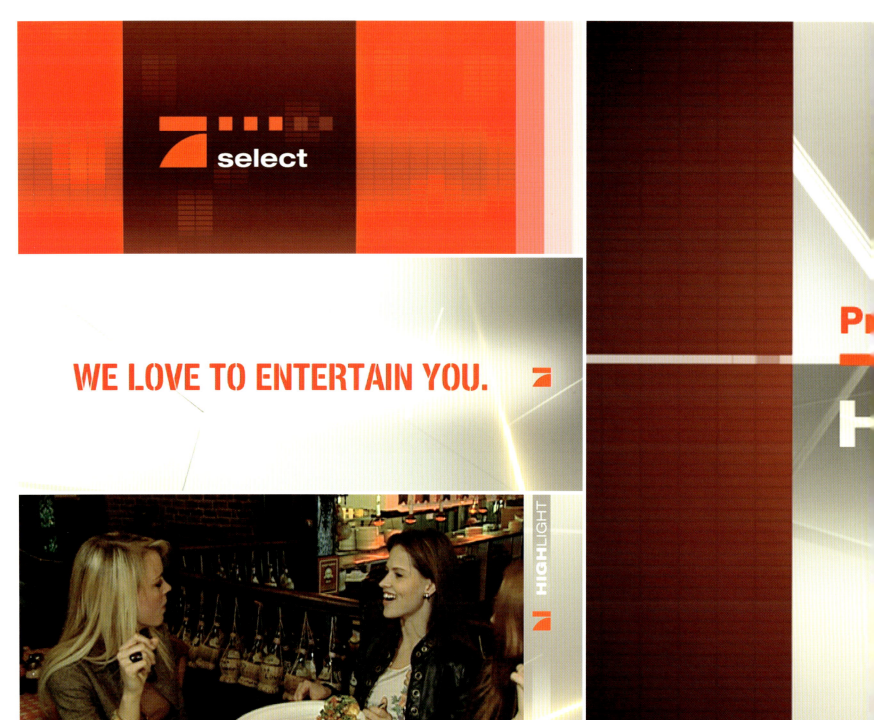

WE LOVE TO ENTERTAIN YOU.

HIGHLIGHT

The screen layout always originates from the logo.
This is the starting point for all the important elements: WE LOVE TO ENTERTAIN YOU (page 130).

BD: How would you sum up the core of ProSieben's design?

PROSIEBEN: ProSieben's design is the visual expression of the ProSieben brand's entertainment remit. Reflecting this key idea, there are fundamental design principles:

The logo in a fixed position in all design and promotion elements as the source of the horizontal entertainment floater, which is the starting point for all the animations, structures the typography and marks the position for all the relevant information.

The entertainment floater's function is key in terms of design, structure and navigation and at the same time embodies the basic principle of the horizontal animations. In addition to these functional aspects, it supports the narrative of the trailers by suggesting different interpretations and thus creates an independent design entertainment.

Float Forward. The fluid transitions between programme elements are a strong feature of ProSieben design; the DNA (Dynamic Nice Animation) creates a seamless flow of design and promotion elements. Everything's constantly moving, there's no start or finish.

Colour was used to awaken emotional responses. There are twelve different colour schemes that transport and strengthen the emotional force of the content. Within the trailer packshots, images are clearly divided into those for rational information-giving, on soothing, purely graphical backgrounds, and those on an emotional level, which use programme shots.

The audio brand also fits in with the mood, forming a unit with the visual elements of the redesign. The mood of the programme is carried over into the audio, but at the same time the audio signals a clear break from the visuals and guides the viewer towards the information in the pack shot.

der Woche

Genre-specific colour schemes and clear divisions create a structured look.
Page 134: Promotion template; page 135: Promotion header.

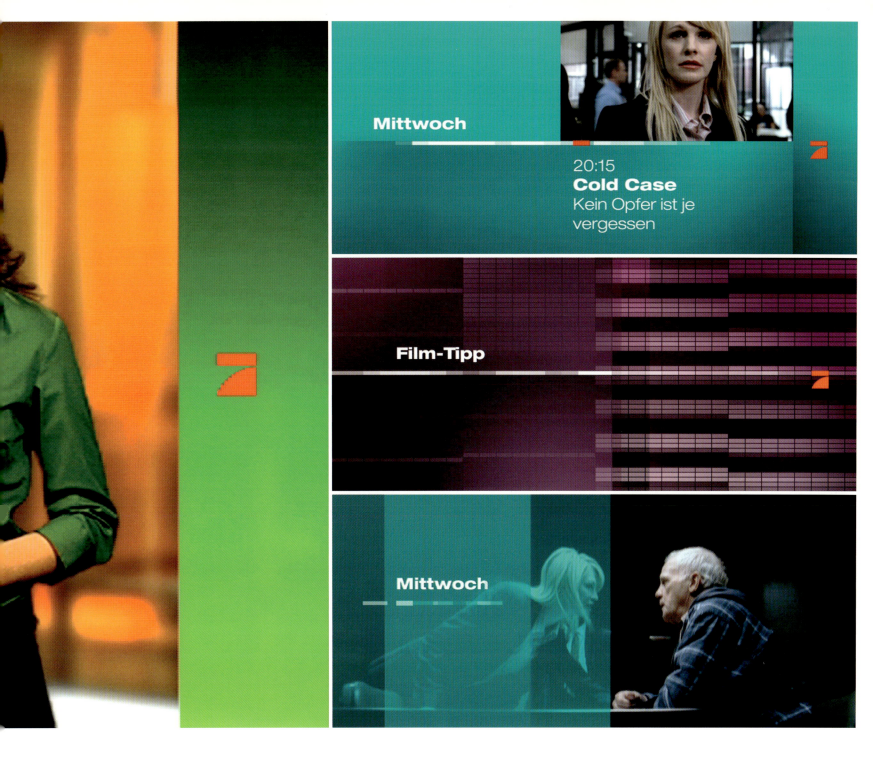

Mittwoch

20:15
Cold Case
Kein Opfer ist je vergessen

Film-Tipp

Mittwoch

BD: You could say that the STAR FORCE campaign was the high point of ProSieben's person-centred branding. How does STAR FORCE work and what does the future hold for it?

PROSIEBEN: ProSieben's STAR FORCE shows the experiences and feelings of the channel's stars. STAR FORCE has a simple remit that is incredibly complex: entertainment. Branding plays a central role and is interpreted in a variety of ways, not just with graphics; set design, styling, make up and set dressing all help create our own, unmistakable star force world, where every frame is a brand message.

Each person from the programmes is portrayed differently, reflecting their own personality, of course always with the right mix of action, glamour, entertainment, irony and a touch of Hollywood – all aspects of the ProSieben brand.

Face branding is the central feature of ProSieben's communication. The faces boost the brand and the programmes and at the same time, the ProSieben brand shines on the stars. It's an effect where each side strengthens the other and creates a real dynamic.

BD: The combination of high quality live action and a reduced graphics world runs throughout all the channel's work. How do you guarantee consistent design and production standards?

PROSIEBEN: The basic remit is to present the ProSieben brand and the various programme brands in as high quality a way as possible. The majority of ProSieben's content (blockbusters, US series) has very high production values, and the elements we generate ourselves have to match those. Elaborate shoots and state of the art design for image campaigns, programme motifs, labels or openers bring these two worlds together and create a cohesive overall impression.

The ProSieben look also applies to the channel's labels – genre and content are perfectly clear
[with no need for additional descriptions].

BD: Integrating bought in content is a constant challenge for a channel, as you have to marry existing design elements with the channel's own image. What have been ProSieben's experiences here?

PROSIEBEN: There's a general consideration about how the programme brands will work with the ProSieben brand. If, for example, blockbusters can boost ProSieben, that's incorporated into the design concept. If that isn't the case, ProSieben always comes first, as the lead brand, and bought in content always comes a clear second.

BD: Design and marketing go hand in hand at ProSieben. How strategic are the channel's design decisions?

PROSIEBEN: We constantly check positioning, brand model, claim and faces to see if they're compatible with the programme's strategic development perspectives. This check-up, combined with quantitative and qualitative market research provides the basis for future decisions about design, image campaigns and programme communication.

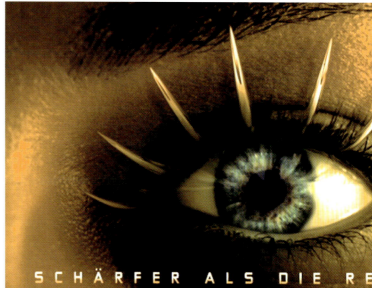

  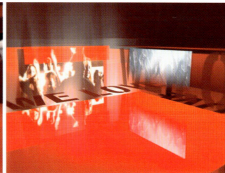

The channel's claim WE LOVE TO ENTERTAIN YOU also appears in different forms on some of the channel's products.

BD: What cycles do you see in today's TV landscape, in terms of design innovations and rebranding? Who's behind this drive for constant re-invention?

PROSIEBEN: The cycles are becoming shorter and shorter. The pace in TV and media has definitely picked up, the advent of digital TV has made it possible for a lot of new channels to enter the market, consumer behaviour for TV and media has really changed. All of this has increased the pressure to keep up.

A typical cycle lasts two to three years, although there's often a few facelifts done and constant efforts to keep things up-to-date.

TV used to be the primary medium for innovation in design, but again here there's been a partial shift towards the internet, where the cycles are noticeably shorter, where there's constantly something new happening somewhere in the world, where there are hardly any constants, where the basic pace is incredibly fast. This shift towards the online world has noticeably increased the pressure on TV brands.

BD: What effect has the increasing use of 16:9 had on the channel's image?

PROSIEBEN: Dealing with 16:9 is still a little way off for ProSieben, thanks to the lack of displays in households. At the moment, ProSieben is still at the knowledge-gathering stage, using a few individual programmes as trials. Since August 13, 2007 the design is compatible with the ratio. We're planning to switch the entire channel's output to 16:9 in 2008.

STAR FORCE has become a successful lifestyle brand!

BD: ProSieben broadcasts various programmes in HD – does that have particular implications for the look and feel?

PROSIEBEN: HD comes with 16:9. In addition, HD is increasingly going to replace film-based technology for promotional and design shoots, which will have an influence on the look and feel.

BD: The close links with other channels in the group (Sat 1, N24, etc.) form an intense part of life at ProSieben. What are the challenges with that and what are the positive impulses?

PROSIEBEN: The close links lead to challenges when several channels are competing in the same market segment. At the same time, that same situation forces the channels to adopt clear and well-defined positions and opens the doors for new potential audience reach through constant cross-promotion.

BD: How does ProSieben see the challenges for brand communication in the increasingly diversifying TV market of the future?

PROSIEBEN: The biggest challenge is maintaining a clear position and sticking to market compatible content and statements over all a brand's platforms. Every platform, every business model has its own rules and logic. Bringing all these under one roof will be the number one challenge for future umbrella brand management.

The interplay between opaque and semitransparent layers helps to structure
the look – examples from promotion, STAR FORCE and info screens.

Typography as architecture on ProSieben. Examples from ProSieben's news designs.

PopStars is one of ProSieben's most successful formats.
Both pages: elements of the format's packaging and the same elements transferred to the studio set.

The STAR FORCE campaign often references other programmes.
This communication strategy is used consistently for on and off air communication. STAR FORCE posters.

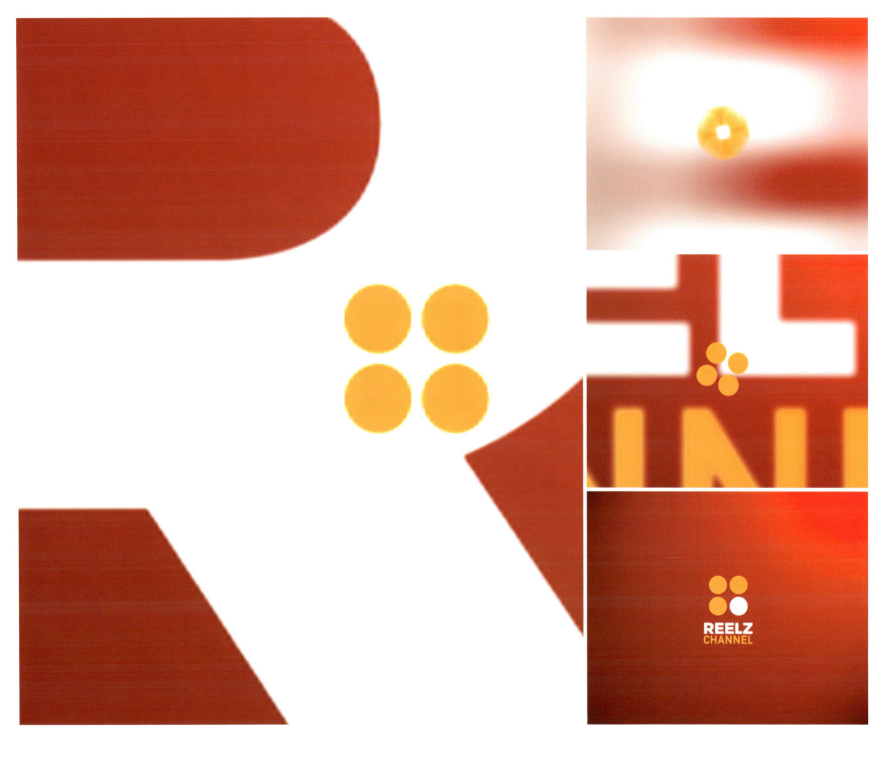

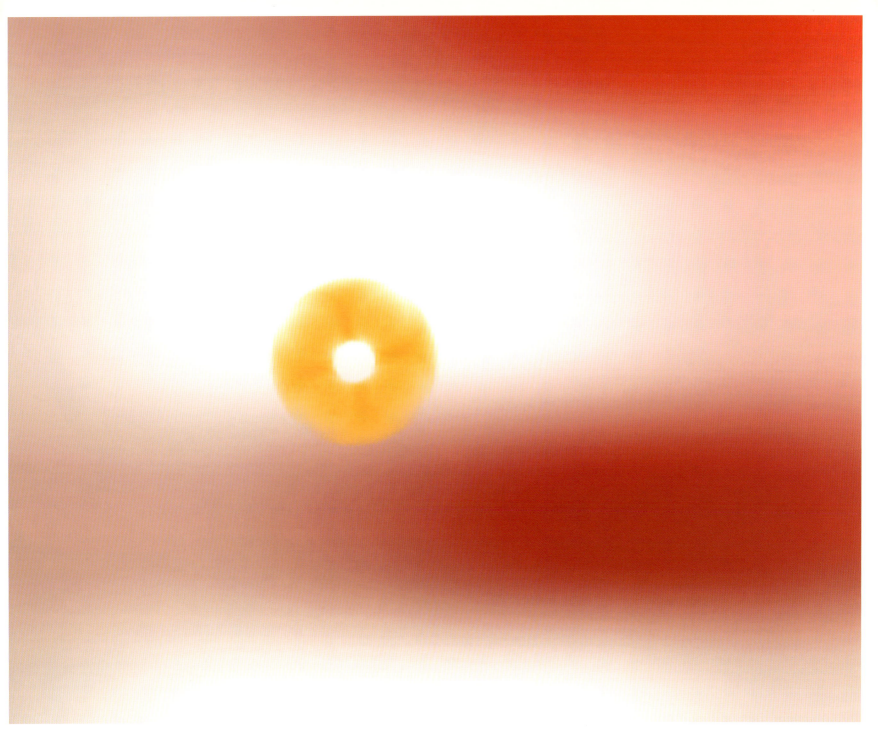

Clarity and simplicity are the basic concepts behind the REELZCHANNEL's corporate design.
Both pages: REELZCHANNEL station ident.

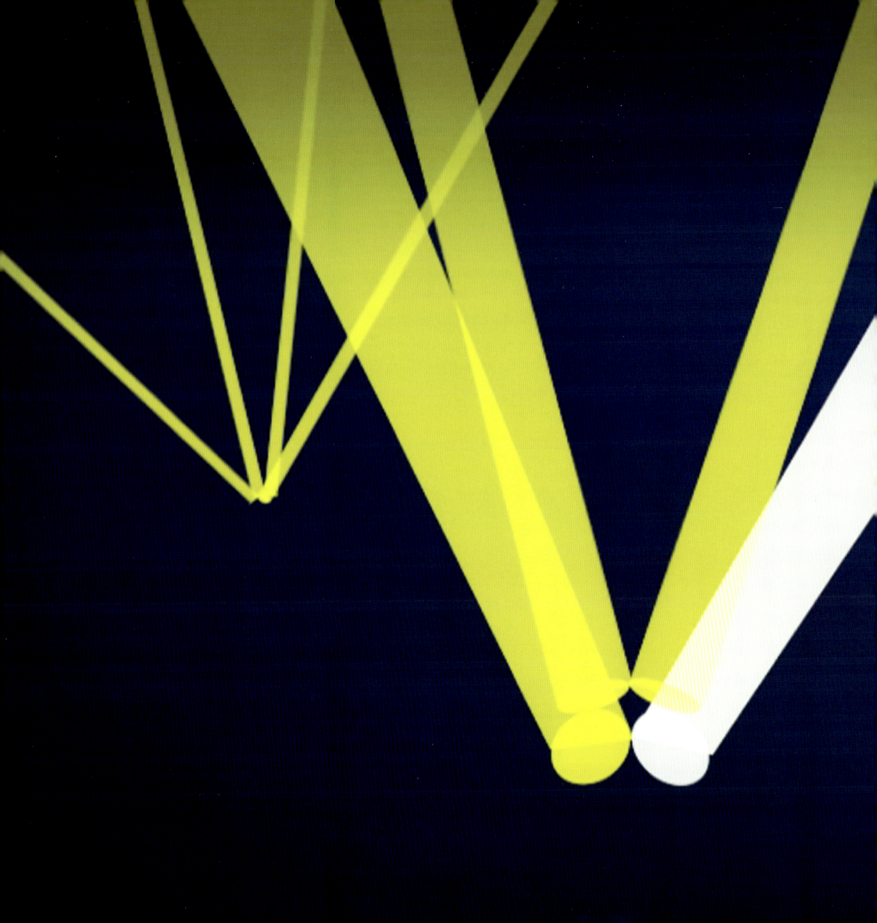

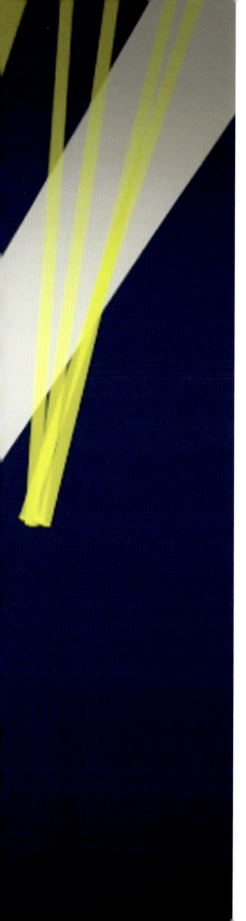

REELZCHANNEL is a cable / satellite channel and website that indulges a movie fans passion for everything and anything about movies. Owned by Hubbard Broadcasting, a third generation family owned broadcasting company, REELZCHANNEL launched September 27, 2006.

REELZCHANNEL is a multi-media destination that provides valuable information movie fans crave, delivered in an entertaining way. The brand is created for movie fans by movie fans – a 24/7 resource that celebrates all aspects of current and contemporary movies in theaters, DVD's, pay per view and video on demand.

REELZCHANNEL doesn't show movies, we make shows about movies. The channel's original programming and content delivers easy access to the kind of material movie fans want most: movie news and movie buzz, trailers, cut scenes, director's notes, cast and crew interviews, reviews, recommendations and behind-the-scenes footage. REELZCHANNEL original programming digs in to every facet of movie making to tell the unique stories behind the scenes and beyond the glitz.

REELZCHANNEL also offers guidance on what to see today, whether it's in theatres or at home. From expert and peer reviews to TV and theater listings, it does everything it can to keep movie fans informed helping them make great movie choices every time. REELZCHANNEL brings everything together under one brand and makes it easily accessible to anyone, anytime, from anywhere.

REELZCHANNEL puts journalistic integrity first. REELZCHANNEL believes there is a movie for everyone, but that doesn't mean we don't recognize when a movie has not lived up to expectations. It's not about trashing anyone or anything — we leave the gossip to others. REELZCHANNEL is committed to digging deeper than anyone else, respecting differing opinions, delivering a fresh perspective and most of all entertaining and informing movie fans.

Described demographically, REELZCHANNEL's target is adults 18-49 who enjoy watching and learning about movies in any medium. They are well-educated, early adapters to new technology, and enjoy being social influencers.

Everyone's a movie fan. We may not all like and appreciate the same ones but that's what makes it interesting. People connect with each other through movies — debating their merits, sharing the experience, recounting favorite scenes, quoting popular lines and even identifying with characters and stories. Movies are an integral part of our lives and our pop-culture.

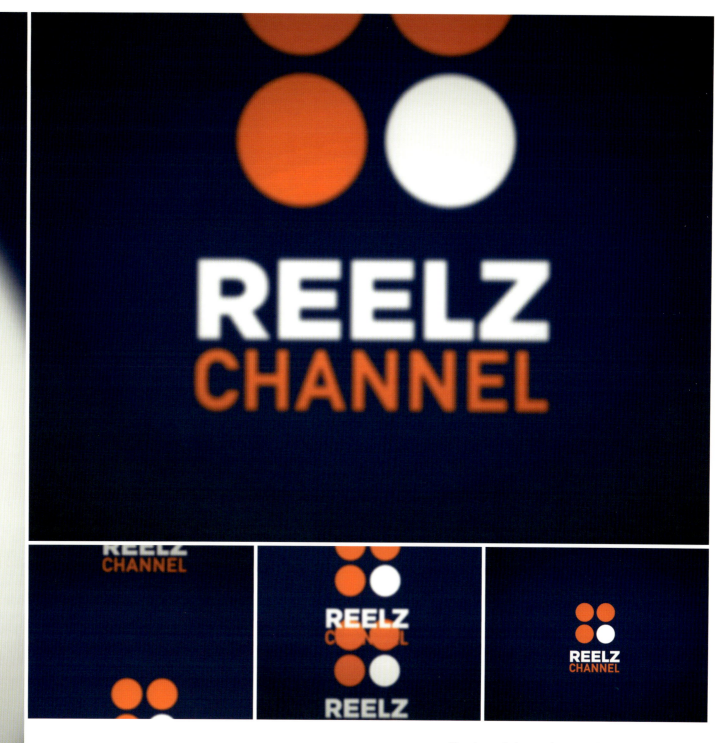

The channel's logo and typography are bold and striking.
Both pages: REELZCHANNEL station ident.

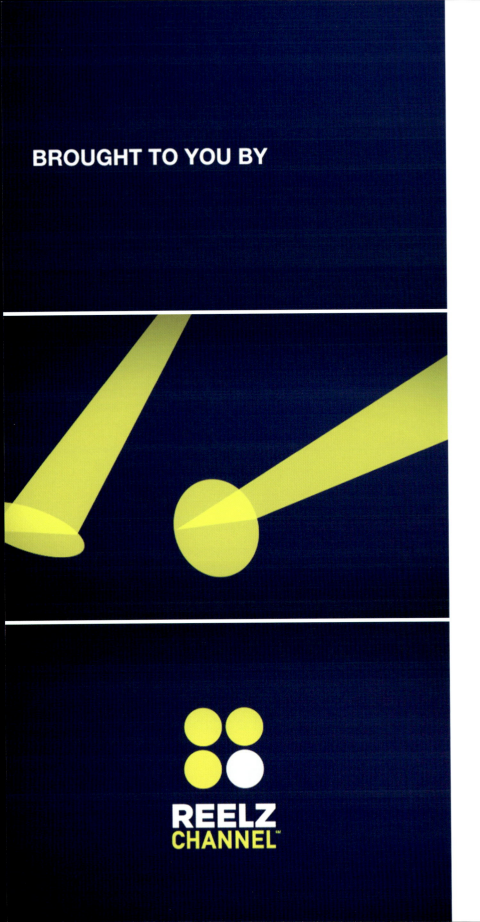

BROUGHT TO YOU BY

The Creative Director of TROLLBÄCK + COMPANY, Jakob Trollbäck (> p.194) kindly answered some questions about BROADCAST DESIGN (BD).

BD: Trollbäck's 2D world offers an antidote to the opulence of Hollywood & Co. What were your motives for depicting the theme in that form?

TROLLBÄCK + COMPANY: There is a rich tradition of great design in Hollywood, but these days it is mostly overrun by the loud noise of promotion. We wanted the channel to be bold and energetic. In order to achieve this you usually have to lose superfluous 3D decoration and textures.

BD: There is also such a thing as economy of design. Where do financial considerations end and issues of content begin?

TROLLBÄCK + COMPANY: Budgets always play a part, but it is complicated to outline exactly how. It doesn't really have an effect on creativity. This was a project that we really wanted to shine, so we invested a lot of time in it.

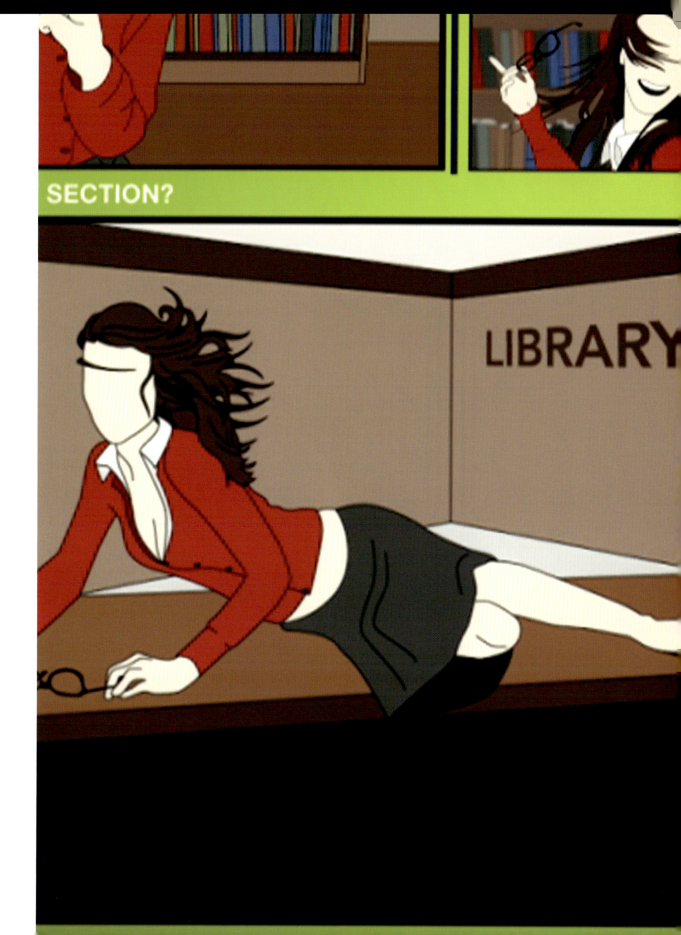

FIG 1. SHHH!

LIBRARIANS

Using the visual language of information design, the network idents offer an ironic twist on film cliches.

BD: The REELZCHANNEL borrows heavily from information design. What role does this path play in the channel's communications strategy?

TROLLBÄCK + COMPANY: Emotionally, we were inspired by the graphic language of film production, like the iconic Dolby and MPAA logos. Then we obviously worked a lot on figuring out the navigation for it all.

BD: The typography for REELZCHANNEL also has a very clean look. How do you stop simplicity drifting off into sheer boredom?

TROLLBÄCK + COMPANY: Boring is when people do stuff just because they can, with little or no reason. The simplicity only relates to the shape of the language; the thinking behind it is everything but. Limiting your language ultimately forces you to be a lot more creative.

A MOVIE MANUAL TO:
CAR CHASES

A MOVIE MANUAL TO:
DEFUSING
A BOMB

A MOVIE MANUAL TO:
DETECTIVE
WORK

Both pages: REELZCHANNEL network idents.

FIG 2. 2 DRINK MINIMUM

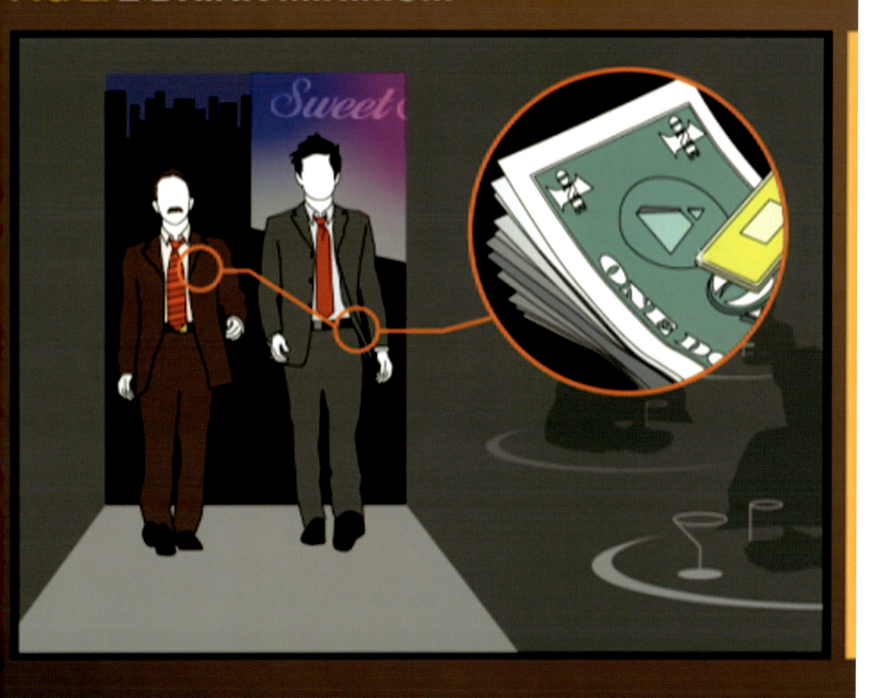

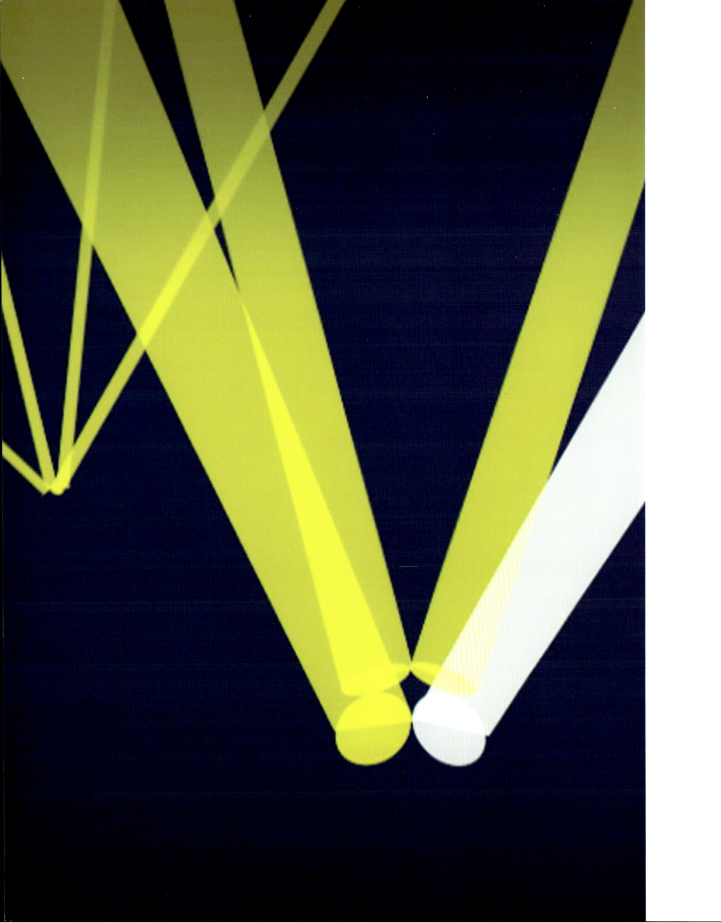

BD: Could you sum up the design principle behind the REELZCHANNEL in a few words?
TROLLBÄCK + COMPANY: To make it bold and fresh. And good!

BD: The increasing fragmentation of the TV market into specialist channels also affects design and branding. What are the effects from Trollbäck's point of view?
TROLLBÄCK + COMPANY: Well, it has actually started to turn the other way now. Even if there is a suggested focus for a channel, they want all the viewers they can get. This actually moves the channels closer to each other.
Specialized channels are much easier to brand than more general channels. You usually have more of a message for them. General channels wants to be everything to everybody, so you're left with some pretty abstract lifestyle-oriented stuff.

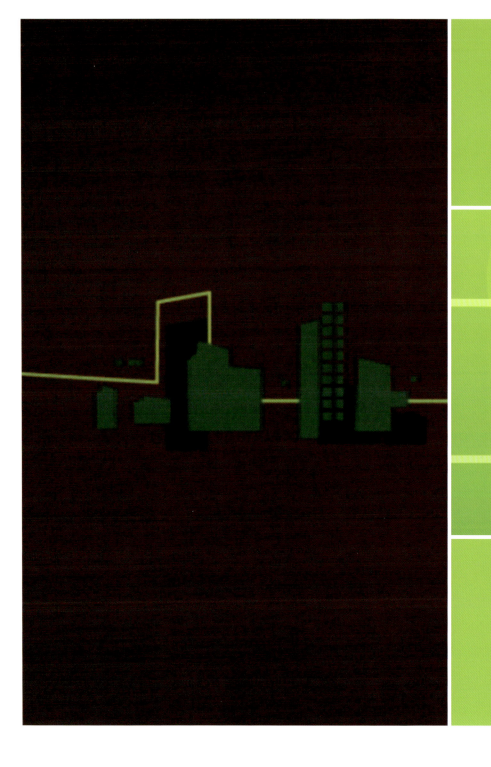

COMING
UP

COMING UP

Dailies

The Directors:
Featuring Martin Scorsese

Hidden Gems

REELZ
CHANNEL

NO. 4294 ®
HIDDEN GEM: NAPOLEON DYNAMITE

This page and opposite left (also overleaf): "Secret's Out" opener.
Opposite page, right: On-Air promotion.

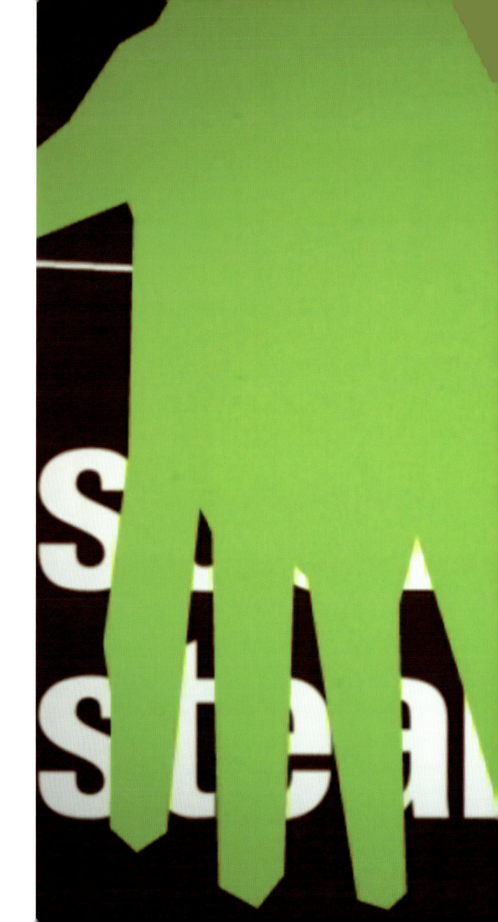

BD: To what extent does a current design for a channel take account of future distribution channels?

TROLLBÄCK + COMPANY: If the design is great, it can be transplanted to many different media channels. You will always have to tweak it. Anyone who believes that you can use the same pieces for Times Square, HD and a mobile phone doesn't really understand how good communication works.

Hidden
GEMS

Secret's Out
with Leonard Maltin

FORGOTTEN
FLi

ers

The latest news from the film world in "dailies" (opener).

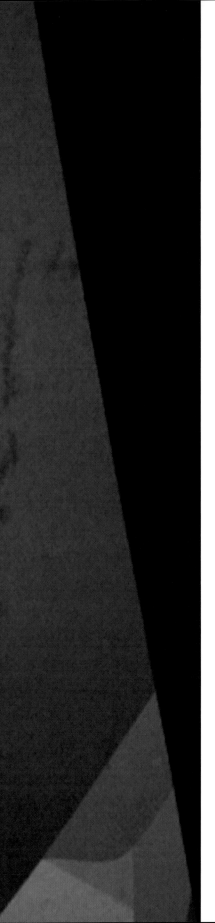

BD: Can you discern local, i.e. national, parameters in broadcast design? Is there such a thing as typical US TV design? **TROLLBÄCK + COMPANY:** Yes, definitely. The European channels can seem totally surreal to American viewers. The tempo is generally much faster on US networks, and as with European vs. American advertising, American networks don't like to take chances. However, since our studio have a majority of European creatives, we do our best to create bold, uncluttered branding and design for American clients.

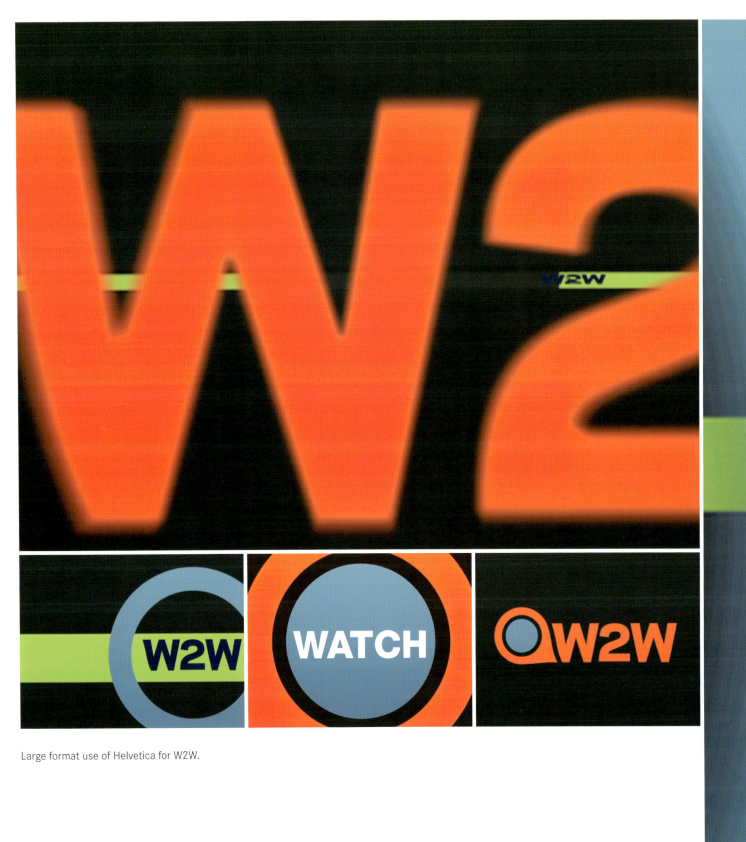

Large format use of Helvetica for W2W.

BD: Is there such a thing as a specific Trollbäck design?

TROLLBÄCK + COMPANY: We always put a lot of effort into finding a strong concept for every project. Our work never has superfluous elements; anything that doesn't add emotion or information is eliminated. The actual designing is usually the easiest part; once you know what you want to convey, most of the work is done.

BD: A statement about the future of TV design?

TROLLBÄCK + COMPANY: There is clearly a future. But it is important to keep in mind that design must add something to people's lives, a feeling, something unexpected or magic and / or a clever way to communicate.

SCORSESE REINER
LEVINSON MANN LEE
GILLIAM CRAVEN FORMAN
REINER SPIELBERG ZEMECKIS JEWISON
LEE SCHUMACHER Mc TIERNAN MARSHALL
LYNE
MANN
SCORSESE REINER
JEWISON
ALTMAN
MANN
SPIELBERG
THE
FRIEDKIN LEVINSON MANN LEE
GILLIAM CRAVEN
REINER ZEMECKIS
MANN LEE SCHUMACHER
CRAVEN FORMAN ALTMAN

DIRECTORS

MARSHALL SCORSESE REINER SPIELBERG
KASDAN FRIEDKIN LEVINSON MANN LEE SCHUMACHER
POLLACK GILLIAM CRAVEN FORMAN ALTMAN LYNE
SESE REINER SPIELBERG ZEMECKIS JEWISON HOWARD

Mc TIERNAN
SPIELBERG
HOWARD
CRAVEN FORM
KASDAN FRI
MANN LEE
TIERNAN MAR
JEWISON HO

ACHER Mc TIERNAN MARSHALL SCORSESE REINER SPI
AN LYNE KASDAN FRIEDKIN LEVINSON MANN LEE
JEWISON HOWARD POLLACK GILLIAM CRAVEN FORMA
ERNAN MARSHALL SCORSESE REINER SPIELBERG Z

The title sequence for "The Directors" quotes film posters.

191

The channel's logo, suggestive of film REELZ, is used as an illustrative element in all media formats.

TROLLBÄCK + COMPANY

ADRESS   302 Fifth Avenue, 14th Floor
                New York, NY 10001, USA

CONTACT   Aimee Przybylski
                www.trollback.com

Trollbäck + Company is a visual and conceptual creative studio producing expressive and purposeful graphics, design and live action for advertising, broadcast, and entertainment.

Led by creative directors Jakob Trollbäck and Joe Wright, the collaborative group of designers and writers launches and rebrands TV networks, creates film titles, environmental installations, print, music videos and TV-commercials.

Trollbäck + Company's trademark approach relies on unorthodox thinking and immersive storytelling, and the belief that a compelling and focused message is essential for any communication to be truly successful.

Founded in 1999, the New York-based studio has received dozens of creative-industry awards, including those from the Primetime Emmy Awards, AICP Show, Art Directors Club, Broadcast Designers Association, D & AD, The One Show, and Type Directors Club.

Clients include TV networks CBS, AMC, HBO, TCM and Sundance Channel; film companies HBO Films, Fox Searchlight and Miramax; and advertising clients Nike, Volvo, Fidelity, and MetLife.

As Trollbäck + Company looks to its future, the goal is to sustain the firm's dynamic blend of high-profile commercial projects as well as its more avant-garde collaborations with emerging and established talents in film, music, architecture, magazines and fashion.

SF

SCHWEIZER FERNSEHEN / SWISS TELEVISION / Switzerland **SF**

The combination of high-quality live action and perfectly
integrated 3D animation is a basic principle of the SF 1 idents.
Both pages: "Glacier" ident.

"SCHWEIZER FERNSEHEN" (Swiss Television) is the largest business unit of SRG SSR idée suisse. With its three channels, SF 1, SF zwei and SF info, its share in 3sat (a channel run jointly by the main networks in Germany, Austria and Switzerland), as well as its internet service www.sf.tv, it makes a major contribution towards fulfilling SRG SSR's remit. Its varied, successful and accessible programming strengthens SCHWEIZER FERNSEHEN's standing among the Swiss German population and forms a significant part of SRG SSR's public broadcasting service. SCHWEIZER FERNSEHEN is divided into eight equal departments: Information, Entertainment, Culture, Sport and Programme Services, as well as the managerial departments Finance and HR, Communication & Marketing and Design.

SF 1 is unmistakably Swiss, predominantly offering informative, entertaining, educational and cultural programming. SF zwei is the channel for sport, series and films as well as modern formats and is aimed at a younger audience. The repeat channel SF info reflects the public's need to choose when they consume TV. The website www.sf.tv offers access to SF's journalistic output, as well as more providing more in-depth and background information. In addition, SCHWEIZER FERNSEHEN is involved with the collaborative channel 3sat, and thus participates in German-speaking televisual culture.

Landscapes and images of urban Switzerland form the backdrops for the idents.
Opposite page: SCHWEIZER FERNSEHEN, pictures from SF 1 station idents "Bridge" and "Lake".

Hansruedi Giger

DJ Bobo

Lauriane
Gilliéron

The Creative Director of SCHWEIZER FERNSEHEN (SF), Alexander Hefter, (> p.232) kindly answered some questions about BROADCAST DESIGN (BD).

BD: SCHWEIZER FERNSEHEN (Swiss Television) is a national institution! Did that mean there were certain rules and taboos for the recent re-design? (By all means say something about the re-design process here!)
SF: We broke a few taboos. For example, we renamed the network, or more accurately made its name much simpler. For the umbrella brand, we changed "SF DRS" (Schweizer Fernsehen der deutschen und rätoromanischen Schweiz, or Swiss Television of German and Romansch Switzerland) into a simple "SF". We're "SCHWEIZER FERNSEHEN". It's obvious that it's a Swiss German-speaking channel.

BD: Switzerland is known for having a very clear design position and the alpine state's typography in particular embodies straight lines and functionality. Does that look feature in the current SF design?
SF: Yes. All the design elements, and especially the studios, are characterised by a clear look. As little as possible, as much as necessary. For the typography we've gone back to Neue Helvetica, the set designs are characterised by a very distinct clarity, with everything reduced to its essence.

SF zwei

Both pages: images from SF zwei station ident "Marco Rima". In contrast to the grand scale of the SF 1 idents, (the second channel) SF zwei focuses on texture and intimacy.

BD: Switzerland is a multilingual country — what does that mean for the SF design?

SF: It's of secondary importance. SF is the network for the German-speaking part of Switzerland, so the country's other languages don't have any influence on the look. The only time we work with the other language channels on design matters is for national projects like the new HD channel or the voting show for Mr. and Miss Switzerland, the national council elections and so on. The main areas where this has an influence is on the typography of the logos or the inserts, which are done in all four languages if necessary.

BD: As we know, audiences today are highly fragmented – we don't talk about homogenous target audiences. How strong is the ability of the on-air design to create identity, and what are the limitations in trying to present a brand for all viewers?

SF: Under the SF umbrella, we have two channels, SF 1 and SF zwei, which are aimed at specific target audiences. Each has its own channel profile and of course the expectations and positioning are reflected in different design worlds and creative strategies. SF 1's programmes, be they factual or entertainment shows, now appeal more strongly to an audience which feels very Swiss; made in Switzerland, for Switzerland. The channel identity is based on Swiss landscape motifs – using the bold SF 1 logo against clear, peaceful panoramas. The audience for SF zwei is more interested in films, series and sport. The new SF zwei identity reflects this, using an emotional and dynamic mix of an animated "zwei" and well-known and young Swiss personalities.

SF zwei station ident's "Serie".

BD: The Swiss TV market is not the largest; it also has to compete with the strong media presence of Germany next door. Did the re-design of the channel reflect the demands of this situation?

SF: Definitely. We know how competitive the market is, especially for films, series and entertainment shows. The look for these kinds of programmes took account of the competitive nature of the industry. The channel's look tells viewers that the content they can expect on SF 1 and SF zwei is just as attractive as that of foreign competitors. The different identities for the two different channels mean we can appeal to a wide range of audience demands.

BD: The design philosophy behind SF in a few short words.

SF: SF gives you Switzerland, SF zwei gives you the world.

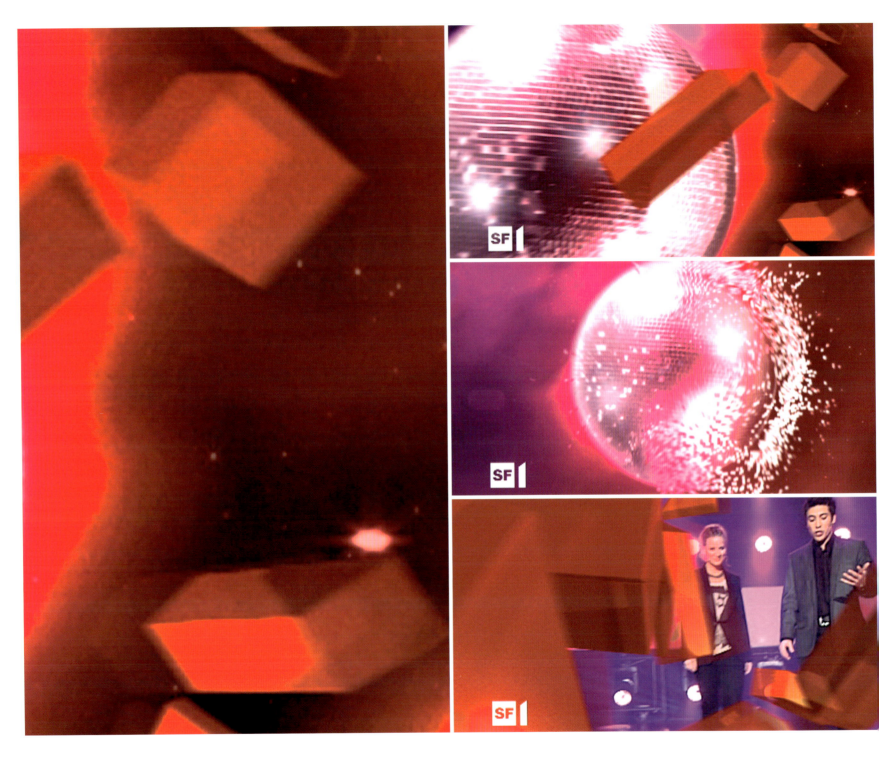

The differences between the two channels becomes clear here.
While SF 1 (opposite page, "Music Star" promotion trailer) has an opulent 3D look,
SF zwei (this page, promo design package) uses a 2D look for its branding.

BD: The news studio in particular confronted the viewer with a fairly radical new approach. Is that one of the design principles of SF? How did the viewers react to it?

SF: The reactions from viewers were mostly, maybe even unanimously, positive. The radical approach worked very harmoniously with the functionality of a news programme. Viewers particularly appreciated the bold studio design and the professional look. A lot of comments that were made said things about being able to be proud of SF news, because it was up to international standards.

BD: Does the SF re-design reflect changes in the world of TV (i.e., new distribution channels, non-linear TV, fragmentation etc.)? Where do future challenges lie and what form will they take?

SF: A very complex question. By using a strong brand architecture and linking the most important programmes, the ones that structure the channel, to the SF umbrella brand, the branding allows these formats to free themselves from the screen but hold on to their brand identity and be clearly recognisable as part of the SF network in a wide variety of vectors and contexts. So the consistency of the brand management means that it will be able to deal with the new and future developments.

Both pages: SCHWEIZER FERNSEHEN, pictures from opener and set design "SF Schweiz aktuell".

BD: The position of the creative director in SCHWEIZER FERNSEHEN is an executive level post – that's quite rare... what are the advantages to this?

SF: The CD always thinks in terms of the whole picture, at the top level, never just at editorial or programme level, always sees the umbrella brand. Of course, decision-making processes work differently if you have certain areas of authority and responsibility.

BD: TV design is no longer seen as mere packaging. What role does the combination of live action and animation play in SF's design? Particularly for the look of the umbrella brand, a lot of importance is attached to creating a look that is as realistic as possible.

SF: That was an aesthetic option that we chose as the artwork for SF 1. We use that principle for the SF 1 idents, the weather and a few other programmes.

Both pages: SCHWEIZER FERNSEHEN pictures from opener and set design "SF Meteo".

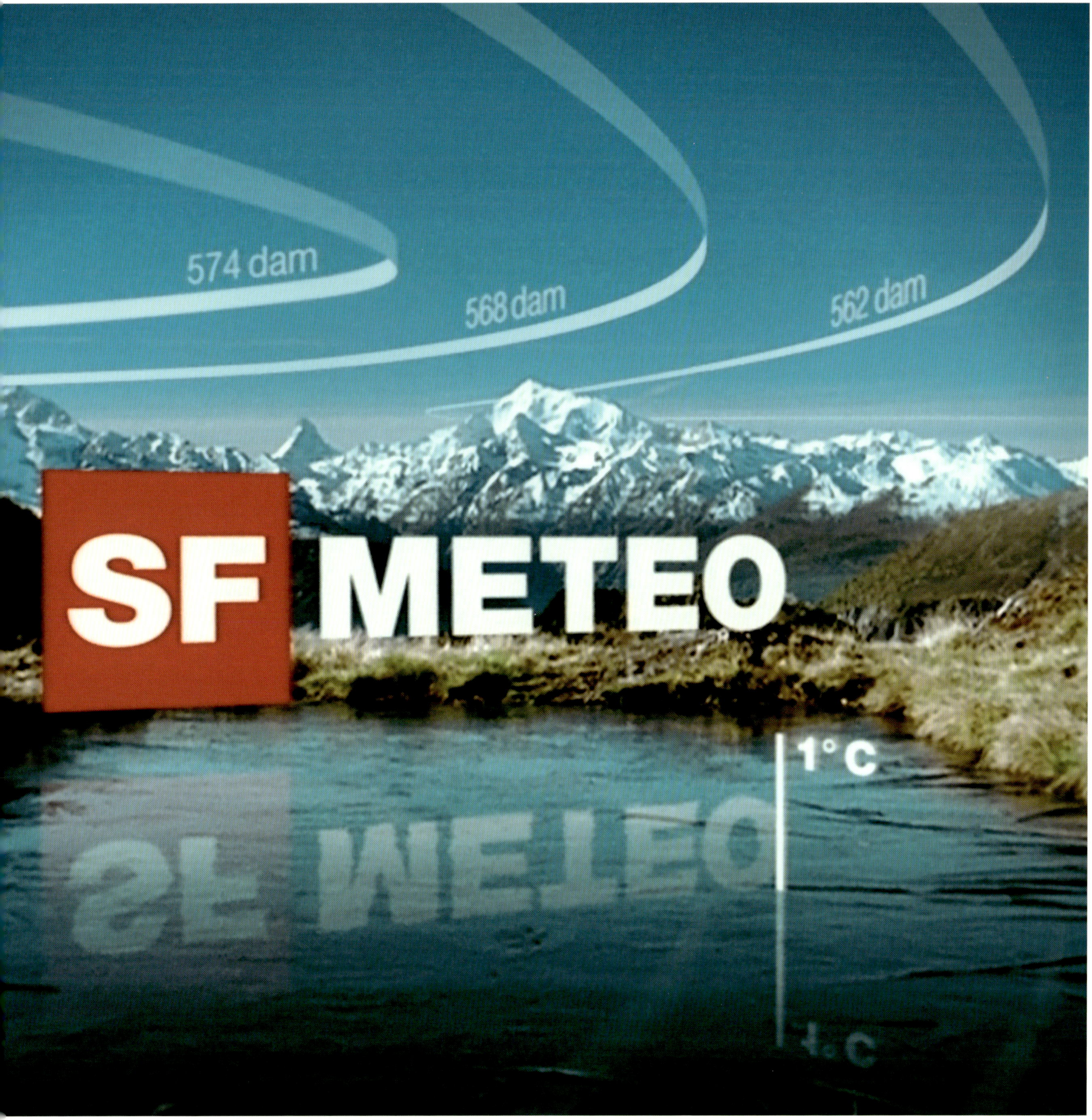
574 dam
568 dam
562 dam
SF METEO
1°C

BD: How do the tools (hard and software) influence the current audiovisual design?

SF: In terms of developing the channel and programme design, those factors don't play a role. The concept is the main thing; choices concerning technology and how to achieve the look are made on the basis of the idea. Of course the channel-specific hardware and software create a certain framework within the programme presentation. Using VizRT as a real-time system for the news for example makes it possible to have a certain form of conveying information, which was developed specifically with the technological possibilities in mind. At the outset, structural decisions were made concerning the hardware and software on the basis of budgetary, operational and functional criteria, and of course these had an influence on the programme presentation.

Leben**live** ^SF

einstein **SF**

SF 1's demands for high audiovisual quality also apply to the formats: elaborate film shoots and image manipulation for the channel's "Einstein" opener.

Both pages: SCHWEIZER FERNSEHEN, pictures from opener "Der Gedankenjäger" and label opener "kino hoch zwei".

The opener for the Swiss lottery draw also uses colours and shapes from the brand roof.
Both pages: SCHWEIZER FERNSEHEN, pictures from opener "Swiss Lotto".

231

SCHWEIZER FERNSEHEN uses clean lines for factual programmes. Format packaging and set design blend
seamlessly. This page, SCHWEIZER FERNSEHEN, picture from set design "Der Club".
Opposite page, SCHWEIZER FERNSEHEN, pictures from opener and set design "Rundschau".

United Kingdom **BBC ONE**

Red Bee also developed a concept that was both open and consistent in terms of colour scheme and look.
Top left: ident "Ring"; all others: ident "Lawn".

BBC ONE is the flagship multi-genre channel for the BBC. In its own words: "BBC ONE aims to be the UK's most valued television channel, with the broadest range of quality programmes of any UK mainstream network. We are committed to widening the appeal of all genres by offering the greatest breadth and depth within them. We will cover national and international sports events and issues, showcase landmark programmes and explore new ways to present specialist subjects".

It is funded entirely by the television licence fee and therefore shows uninterrupted programming with no commercial advertising. The multi-genres include event and ongoing drama, landmark factual series, sit-back entertainment, live events, news and regional news. It holds a share of around 22 percent of total television viewing in the UK, but its peak audiences can reach over 20 million people. Following the rebrand in October 2006, this year it was awarded Broadcast Magazine's "Channel of the Year" with the judges commenting: "At a time when all major terrestrial broadcasters are facing questions about how fast and far their share of viewing will fall, BBC ONE has shown it can deliver mass entertainment". Key popular programmes include Planet Earth, Doctor Who, Strictly Come Dancing, the Olympic Games, The Apprentice, Life on Mars, Bleak House, Eastenders, Spooks, Little Britain, The Vicar of Dibley and the World Cup.

To reflect the countries within the United Kingdom that the channel is available in, BBC ONE has individual services for Scotland, Wales and Northern Ireland. The channel's visual identity for these services is largely the same as the version used in England, save for the inclusion of the relevant country name below the main BBC ONE logo.

In the English regions, the BBC has regional news and current affairs programme opt-outs as well as a limited amount of continuity for the English regions. During such regional opt-outs, the region name is displayed as with the national variations, in smaller characters beneath the main channel logo.

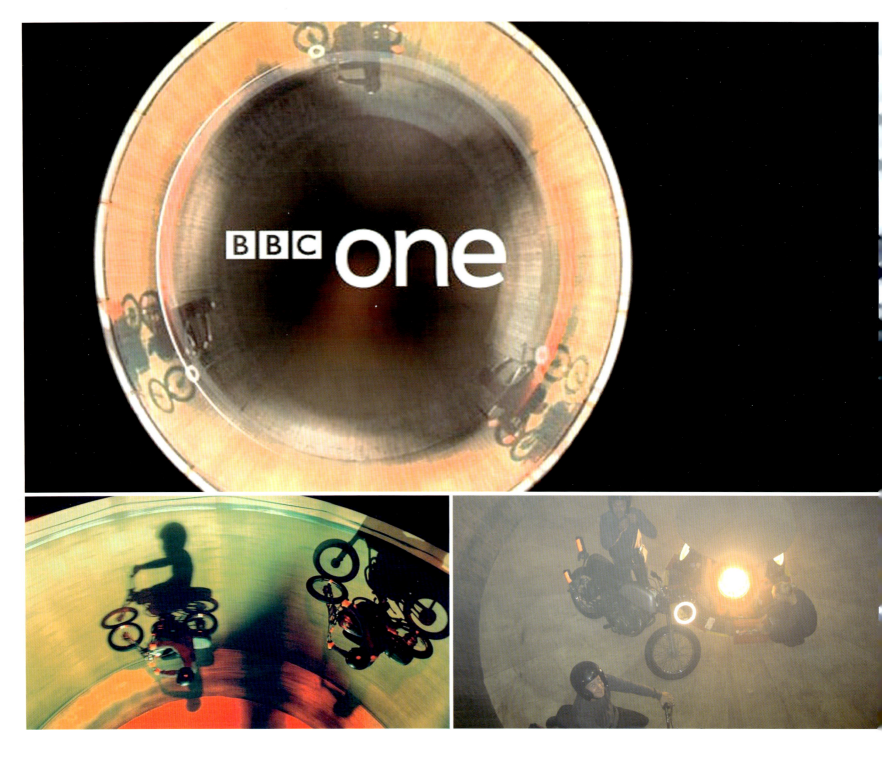

"Bikes" (opposite page) turns a ride round a velodrome into a cosmic experience!
This page: the storyboard for the "Bikes" ident.

241

The Executive Creative Director of Red Bee Media, Charlie Mawer, (> p. 272), kindly answered some questions about BROADCAST DESIGN (BD).

BD: You have to tread extremely cautiously when you're re-branding as strong a brand as BBC ONE... How did you manage to keep the balance between innovation and maintaining the traditional brand values?

RED BEE: It is a balancing act, but Naomi Gibney, our BBC marketing client, was committed to moving the channel's image forward. One of the ways you can do this is by demonstrating genuine creativity and the highest standards of production in every ident. We wanted an idea that was flexible for us not to be boxed into, effectively repeating the same visual device and the same look and feel over and over again. Even the most hardened traditionalist viewers respond to wit and charm and inventiveness, and research has shown that the most seemingly leftfield of the idents have proved the most popular.

Our use of the circle was a strong nod to the heritage of BBC ONE however. The very first examples of a moving channel brand from the 50s used the circle as an emblem for BBC ONE.

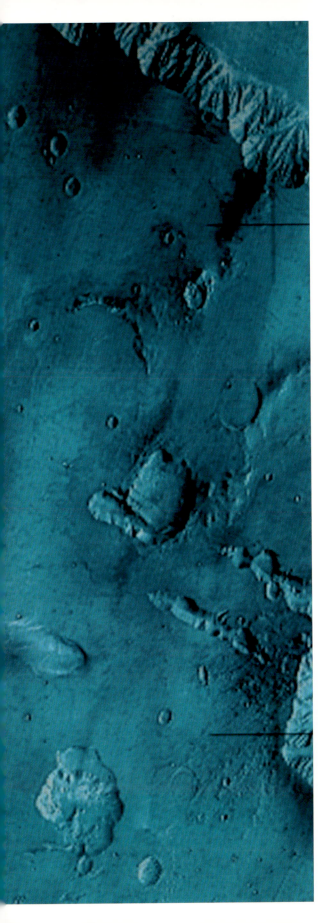

BBC ONE has even branded the surface of the moon!
Red Bee uses the visual language of modern space travel for the "Mission Control" ident.

BD: Were there strong strategic base parameters for the job? Is TV design even capable of creating a precise positioning and addressing a target audience?

RED BEE: Absolutely. The days of design being based on a creative whim are long gone. Strong strategic insight and a rigorous analysis of a brief underpin any project we work on, and BBC ONE was no exception. TV design will always only be one element of communicating a precise positioning. The content of the brand itself should be the strongest tool to shift perceptions, but TV design does represent the brand in its purest, most condensed form and therefore its role is critical. For BBC ONE the structural strategic foundation was the positioning of BBC ONE as a channel that brought people together, both at a national and a familial level. In a world of increased audience fragmentation, Peter Fincham, the BBC ONE channel controller, outlined his vision for the channel as responding to the basic human need for shared moments.

BD: In the fiercely competitive market, the unique nature of the brand is of great importance for the broadcaster. In a few words, what would you say were the essential building blocks of BBC ONE's design?

RED BEE: The circle as an emblem of togetherness; a moment of magic and creativity that leads to the circle; everything stems from BBC ONE – the logo is literally the heart of the channel with the new onscreen presentation system – and everything comes together as one around it

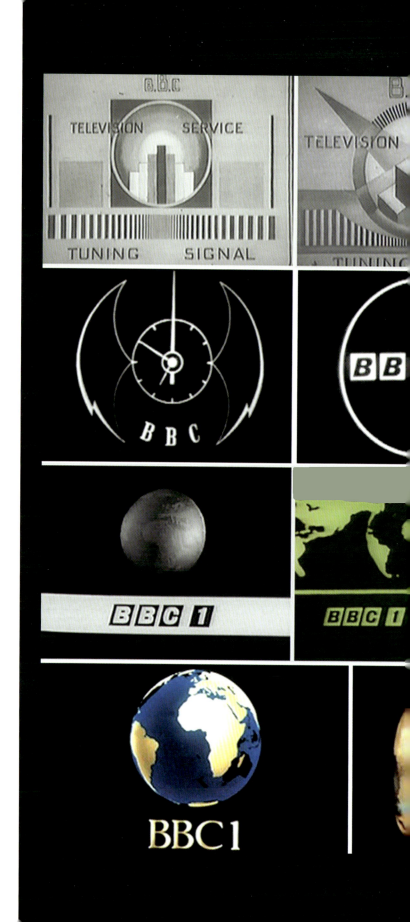

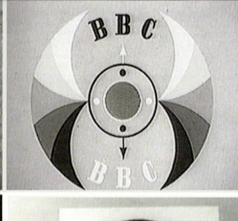

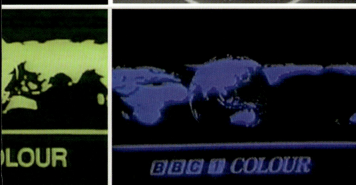

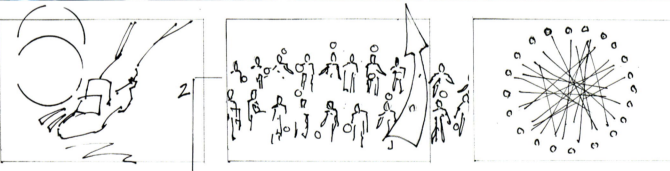

The concept of the circle suggests the closed nature of the singular as well as the
unity of a group – it celebrates the beauty of collaboration as well as the beauty of a simple shape!
Both pages: Football ident.

BD: The logo was reworked as part of the recent rebranding (Jason Smith / Fontsmith). How important are design details like this? Is the consumer even aware of them?

RED BEE: A change in logo and font is never going to be an instant source of reappraisal for the consumer, but as part of any overall branding job they are vital tools for communicating personality. The playful kicks and curls within the unique font are perfectly in tune with the tone of the idents, whilst the perfect circle of the "o" reflected the overall idea of people coming together as one. The move from upper to lower case was an easy decision to make as it is an instantly warmer and more approachable design.

BD: Sound design is very important for the effect of all the elements. How did Red Bee manage the interaction between image and sound during the development process?

RED BEE: From very early on we wanted the sound and music design to play a crucial role. We wanted it to be flexible enough to match the range of moods and tones we were striking with the visuals, whilst retaining a signature tune that over the years would emerge as a strong but subtle branding device. This becomes particularly important when cross trailing BBC ONE content on radio networks for example.
We had an amazing choice of composers and bands pitch for the job, and eventually selected a single composer – Imran Hanif – who was capable of working with our offline pictures to create unique musical treatments with a common theme.

BBC Moon.

1

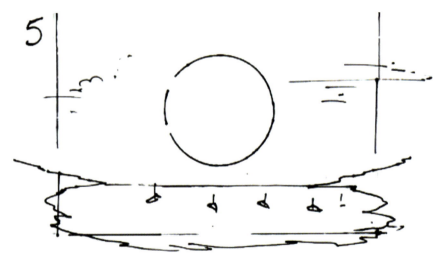

5

Poetic perfection of form: "Moon" ident (both pages).

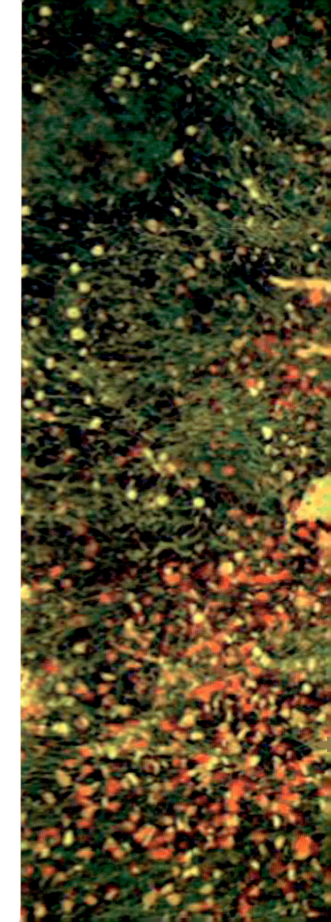

BD: The channel belongs to a family of channels. Does that create specific demands for the brand design?

RED BEE: Yes and no. We needed to be aware of BBC ONE's place within a portfolio of channels, both in its strategic positioning and its design solution. The end result had to be complementary to other services whilst confident of its own position. On a purely practical level, the logo had to work as a patch within portfolio communications such as channel line-up messages, end credit squeezes, website pages and so on. The colour red was also retained as a BBC ONE property partly because of the need to maintain a portfolio design palette.

BD: The BBC is state-owned (but quasi-autonomous). What effect does that aspect have on the visual representation?

RED BEE: The BBC isn't actually state owned. So don't really understand this question. It is paid for by a licence fee. The BBC has the same professional disciplines as any other broadcaster so I don't think that the ownership is a factor. Obviously we are careful to ensure all of our audiences are catered for and represented but that is the challenge for any mainstream broadcaster, not just the BBC.

The BBC ONE idents constantly offer new and surprising interpretations
of "the circle", establishing the central element of the corporate design in a variety of ways.
Both pages: "Snowball" ident.

BD: Is there such a thing as typical British TV design? What are the particular features of the British market in terms of design and branding?

RED BEE: I don't think British TV design has "a typical look". It has a history of using idents as longer films, which really communicate a brand essence, more than many other parts of the world. I think it's possibly true that we use humour more than some other international areas, but really in 2007 any attempt to generalise about national markets feels pretty false and parochial.

BD: The BBC has a very innovative positioning in terms of new media channels, even proclaiming the death of classical TV distribution. In this context, how are channel brands going to develop? Will they even exist any more?

RED BEE: Channel brands are going to be here for a long time to come. There is convincing evidence that people still enjoy the role of editor and trusted guide that a strong channel brand provides. Whilst the trend towards "passion channels" (where people cluster around their genres of interest) is inevitable in a multi-channel world, and a very long term view of on demand will play strongly into programme brands strengths, the fact that the five terrestrial channel brands in the UK (which are all multi-genre) still combine an audience share of around 70 percent suggests that their demise has been greatly exaggerated.

In "Forest" we visit woodland inhabitants, real and imaginary, in their natural setting.
This ident shows that as well as genre-specific references, the BBC ONE idents can also be used to address target audiences and specific age groups.

BBC

BBC. SURFER.

1

2
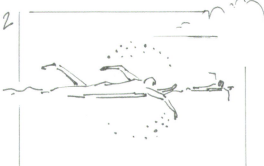

3

4.

BD: To what extent does BBC ONE's programming correlate to the audiovisual image?

RED BEE: We try to make the corollary more about mood than about specific genres. So we chose idents that could work into a wide range of content. From Saturday night entertainment and broad comedy, through to dramatic action and natural history. From daytime to late night, from major sporting events to music and dance. We need idents that can also play into challenging news and current affairs stories. Ones that have an air of neutrality to balance very intrusive and comical ideas.

BD: The fusing of live action and computer animation and the labour-intensive postproduction create something like a new (audio)visual reality. How much control do you have over the intended effect?

RED BEE: We believe firmly in collaboration with experts in their fields to produce the best possible outcome. Like the ideal relationship between a client and an agency, it is all about choosing the right partner and then giving them the space and trust to deliver the right end product. Specifically with regard to the mix of animation and live action, we worked with two of London's leading post-production houses – CFC Framestore and Clear. Our producers who are extremely experienced in high end post involved them from early on in the creative process, and we pushed their technical expertise into new areas, whether it was filming for the first time ever with a 35 mm camera mounted on a jetski for surfing, the 3D animation of Hippos or detailed model making for Mission Control.

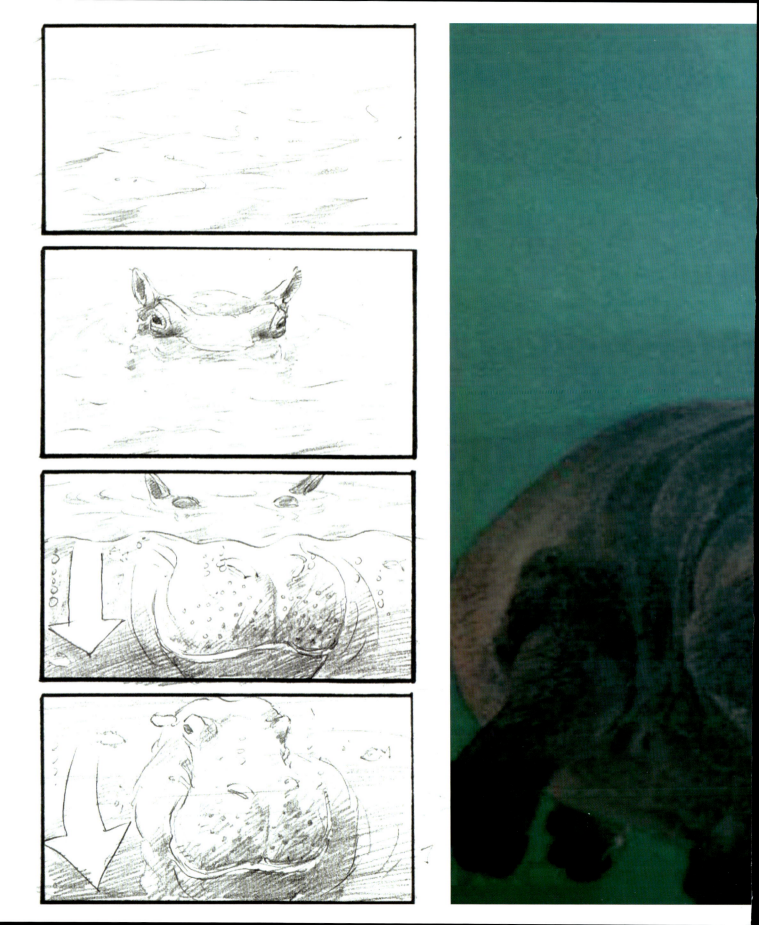

Live action and computer animation are seamlessly blended
as seen in the "Hippos" water ballet (pages 264, 265) – the intention is to leave the audience guessing
what is really possible and what is "the power of television".

The On-Air promotion also uses the concept of the circle, so the central element of BBC ONE's
branding is featured again here. Both pages: BBC ONE promotion.

Thursday 8.00
The Inspector
Lynley Mysteries

BBC one

BBC one

Both pages: BBC ONE On-Air promotion.
The circle element is used as a background or in the wipes.

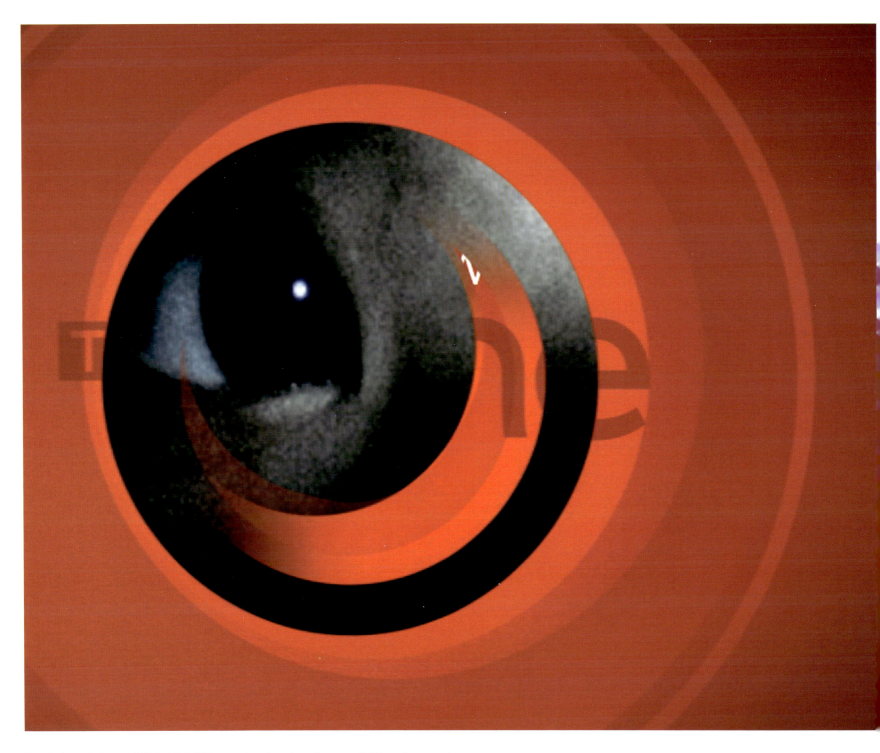

Developing a font especially for BBC ONE guarantees broad media compatibility and represents
another unique element of BBC ONE's corporate identity.
This page: on air promotion; opposite page: BBC ONE font and podcast screen.

alternative l/c 'a'

alternative l/c 't'

slight flare reflecting
personality from logo.

retaining consistent circular idea

slight flare reflecting
personality from logo.

subtle curvature of the ear of the
character, allowing more air into the shoulder
and creating ownership and personality

circular outside shape
slightly more squareness on the inside

broad shouldered character
retaining consistency with l/c "o"

circular proportioned and
wide enough to retain balance
with l/c "o"

logo

font (bold weight)

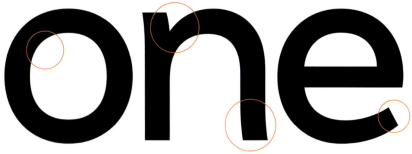

notice the change of width of the letters
From the logo to the font. This is to get line
lengths and program names running to optimum
length whilst retaining character.

Tonight 9.00
Trawlermen

BBC one

MENU

RED BEE MEDIA

ADRESS	Broadcast Centre,
	201 Wood Lane
	London, W12 7TP, UK
PHONE	+44 20 8495 5710
FAX	+44 20 8495 5710
CONTACT	jeff.conrad@redbeemedia.com
	www.redbeemedia.com

"Creativity requires the courage to let go of certainties" – Nearly thirty years after his death, Erich Fromm's words still resonate, more so in the world of broadcast media, where success or failure increasingly depends on the ability to challenge all preciously held assumptions – even if, as Marshall McLuhan famously suggested, they were 'useless' in the first place.

Indeed, in the phrase 'broadcast media' itself, there's an assumption crying out to be demolished. The digital media landscape is changing rapidly and if 'broadcasters' are to thrive, they have to reach out beyond their traditional universe and grab audiences wherever they can – through broadband, IPTV, on demand, mobile etc. Originally a commercial subsidiary of the BBC, reborn as Red Bee Media under new ownership in 2005, and now with offices around the world, our experience in all aspects of content promotion, branding, delivery and navigation is pretty much unrivalled.

For whilst we recognise that at the heart of every successful brand there remains a simple truth or a great idea, the ability to express that idea through new and ever changing forms of media is vital and a non-negotiable demand of the creative process. It's no longer enough to simply tell consumers what to do and hope they meekly comply. We have to engage with them across a host of different technologies and platforms - empowering them to act as advocates on behalf of the brand.

So whether we're designing an international channel identity, a user interface for an IPTV provider, or a WAP site that integrates with a TV drama campaign, the combination of a beautiful concept, smart strategic thinking and a deep understanding of multi-platform technologies is the ideal recipe for brand alchemy.

All of the above challenges the concept of a traditional communications company. And although we wouldn't claim to have reached new media nirvana, we firmly believe that we possess the required mix of creative, editorial and technical skills to help us get there.

sundance
CHANNEL®

Sundance Channel / USA **SUNDANCE CHANNEL**

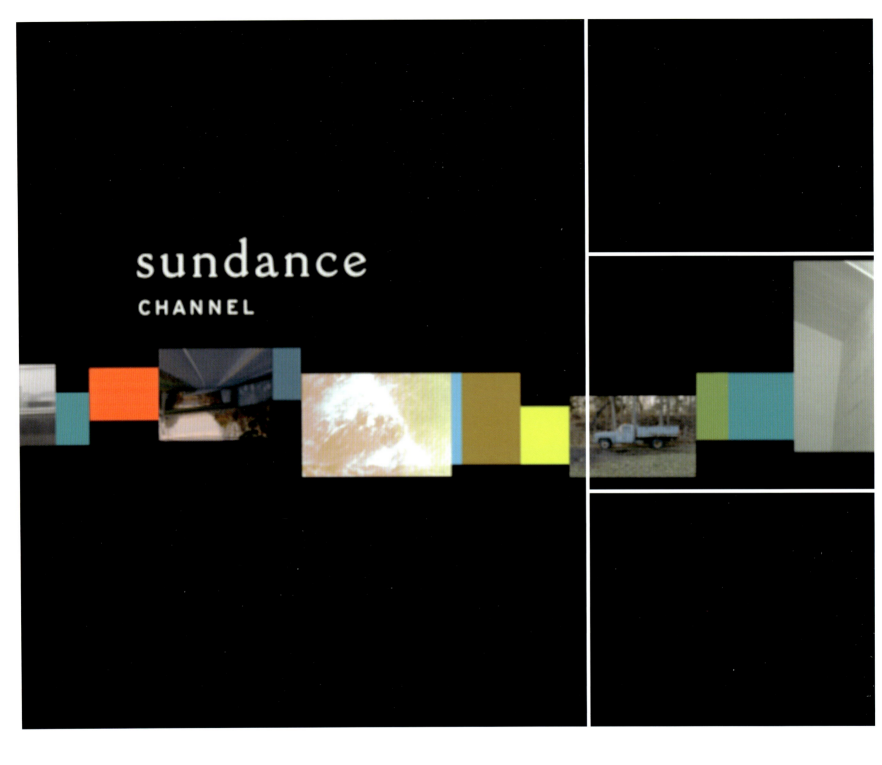

a

for

Sundance Channel, an offshoot of the Sundance Film Festival, pursues a programming schedule with a very independent point of view. This is supported by a visual purity and unconventional audio. Both pages: "For A Change" ids.

sundance
CHANNEL

Under the creative direction of Robert Redford, Sundance Channel is the television destination for independent-minded viewers seeking something different. Bold, uncompromising and irreverent, Sundance Channel offers audiences a diverse and engaging selection of films, documentaries, and original programs, all unedited and commercial free. Launched in 1996, Sundance Channel is a venture of NBC Universal, Showtime Networks Inc. and Robert Redford. Sundance Channel operates independently of the non-profit Sundance Institute and the Sundance Film Festival, but shares the overall Sundance mission of encouraging artistic freedom of expression.

for a change.

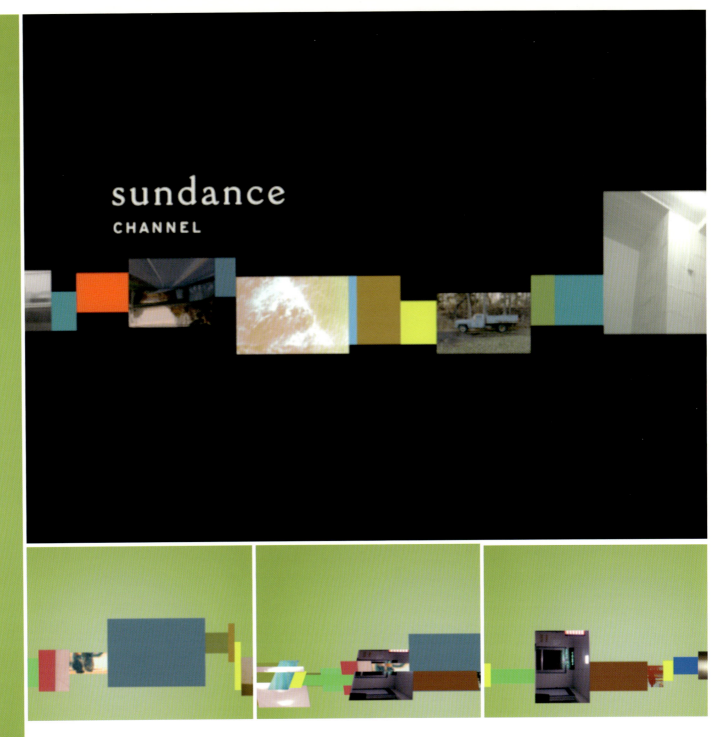

"For A Change" reflects the channel's ethical and ecological awareness as much as the content of its programmes.
Both pages: "For A Change" ids.

SVP Branding, On-Air & Creative Services, Sundance Channel Sarah Barnett, kindly answered some questions about BROADCAST DESIGN (BD).

BD: What role does the festival of the same name play for Sundance Channel – how much interaction is there?
SUNDANCE CHANNEL: Sundance Channel and Sundance Film Festival share the same independent spirit and mission to nurture new ideas and voices, along with the objective to connect independent storytelling with an audience. In terms of direct interaction, as the official television network of the Sundance Film Festival, Sundance Channel covers the ten days of the Festival with daily broadcasts and comprehensive updates both on-air and online.
Also, Sundance Film Festival feeds films and filmmakers into the Channel's content, as we acquire a large number of films from the Festival.

BD: The Channel's content is challenging and unconventional. Does that affect the channel's branding?
SUNDANCE CHANNEL: Challenging and unconventional are characteristics that people expect from the brand and our tagline "for a change" reflects that. The branding does express this kind of artistry and innovation but at the same time it also acts as an accessible bridge to our content. In our branding we strive for a high standard of creativity while also making the channel feel inviting and entertaining.

sundance
CHANNEL.

"The Green": Sundance Channel's space reserved exclusively for environmental issues.
Both pages: "The Green".

BD: It's safe to assume that Sundance Channel's audience is relatively highly educated, in keeping with the programming. Does that mean that they have a more reflective or more open way of responding to design?

SUNDANCE CHANNEL: We definitely have a design savvy, sophisticated audience. They are certainly open to new ideas, and as they like to be a little ahead of the curve, we think that they are open to arresting, innovative communication on all levels, including design. That's not to say that we strive always to be high concept in our branding. Sometimes the most simple form of expression, well executed, is the smartest route and most well received solution.

BD: Is it possible to sum up the channel's design philosophy in a few words?

SUNDANCE CHANNEL: We believe in original creative vision and smart execution – our tagline is 'for a change' so we are curious to explore authentic and innovative ways for design to do its job.

Both pages: "The Green".

for a change.™

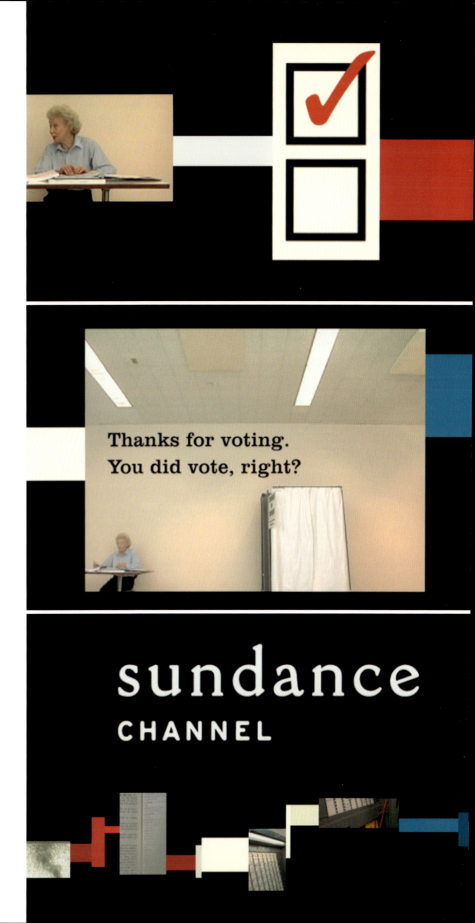

BD: If you compare the US and European TV markets, do you notice particular differences?
SUNDANCE CHANNEL: Europe is more rooted in a classic design aesthetic that has been reflected in broadcast design, while US TV branding comes from a more "show biz" place, but maybe the two continents are learning from each other and moving a little closer together as there is more sharing of content, either through format deals or acquisitions.

BD: Do these differences also apply to Sundance Channel, or would you say that the concept you use (in terms of content as well as design) make you a bit of an exception in North America?
SUNDANCE CHANNEL: We are one of those channels that could exist in either North America or Europe. We are a bit of a hybrid.

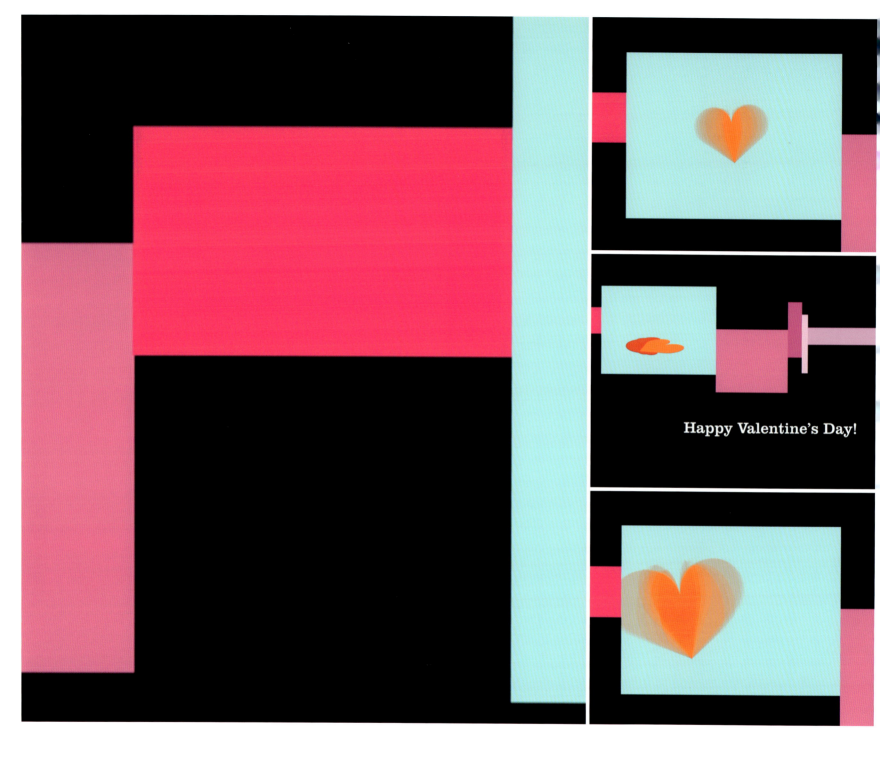

Happy Valentine's Day!

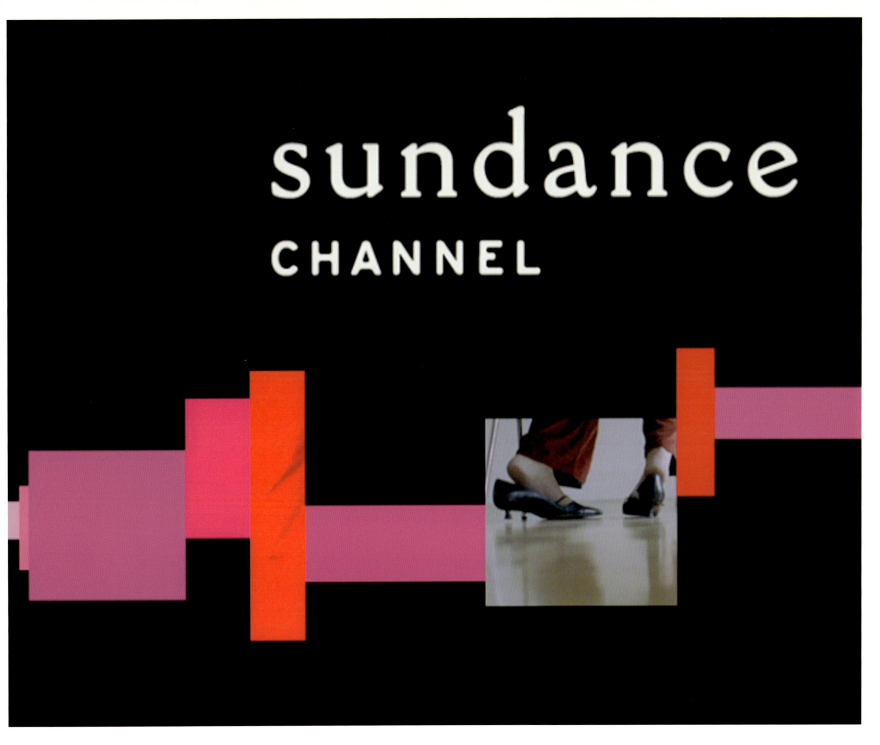

Sundance Channel's design uses simple methods,
but it's always done with a sense of humour and the style is highly recognisable.
Both sides: idents for "Valentine's Day".

BD: How do the creative processes in the channel function – from briefing to the final version?

SUNDANCE CHANNEL: The channel is pretty small so decisions are made quickly. For smaller projects the brief circulates internally from our marketing team to the creative team. Two or three creative directions are presented and one is selected. Approvals are sought from the General Manager / EVP Programming & Creative Affairs and the EVP Marketing and Branded Entertainment. On bigger Channel projects, we will have pitches from outside design companies, and approvals may be circulated to higher levels within the Channel.

BD: Does Sundance Channel make the majority of projects with its own team, or is a lot of work contracted out?

SUNDANCE CHANNEL: See above: the majority of projects come from our small boutique internal creative agency; for bigger projects, outside broadcast design companies will be invited to pitch.

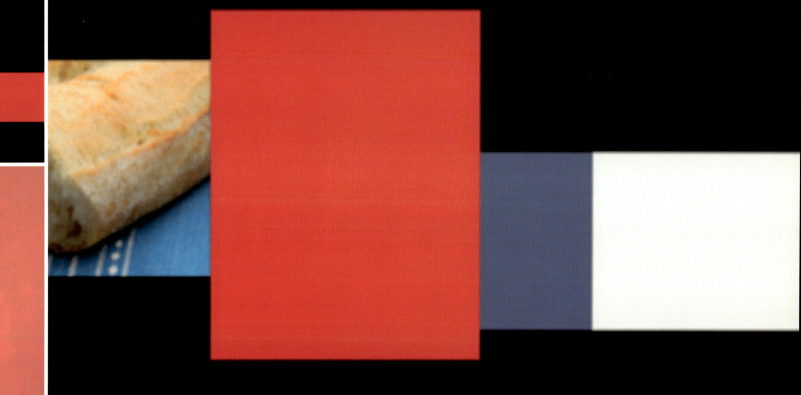

sundance

CHANNEL

h, happy b

ll day.

e day.

The journey is the destination – both sides: "trail" ident.

sundance
CHANNEL

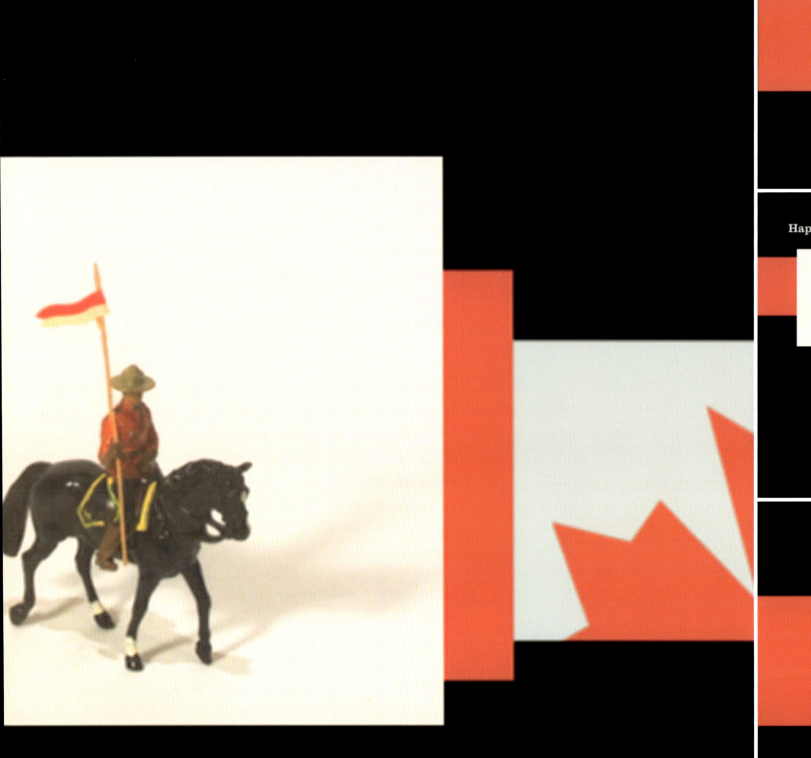

Happy Canada

Happ

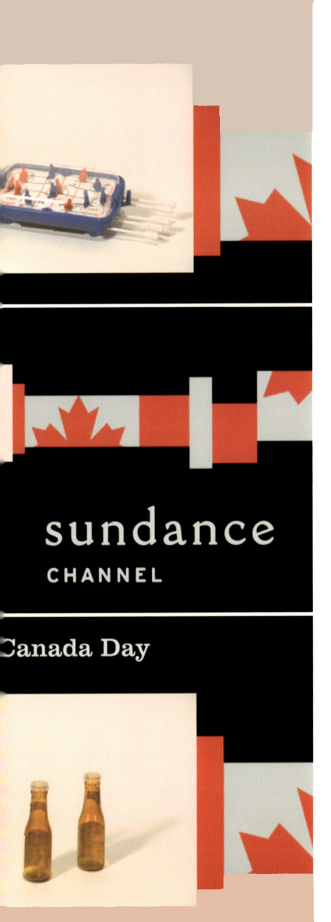

sundance
CHANNEL

Canada Day

BD: Is being based in New York particularly important in terms of the creative environment? (... or, in the age of globalized communication and possibly also international design language, is that not important any more?)

SUNDANCE CHANNEL: Everywhere provides inspiration and we are surrounded by incredible talent in New York City. But just like everybody else, we draw on talent from everywhere, including outside the US.

BD: There's a lot of discussion at the moment about the changes to established distribution models - e.g. IPTV, to give just one example that's on everyone's lips. Is this also an issue for Sundance Channel and what are the effects of this on design and communication strategies?

SUNDANCE CHANNEL: We apply our core qualities of smart, creative and authentic to all new platforms and modes of distribution. Of course the particular functionality of new distribution models requires new design executions, but conceptually we always try to stay true to the heart of our brand.

299

One of the channel's features is its scurrility. Far from the mainstream, the "Orsino Players" play their own tune...

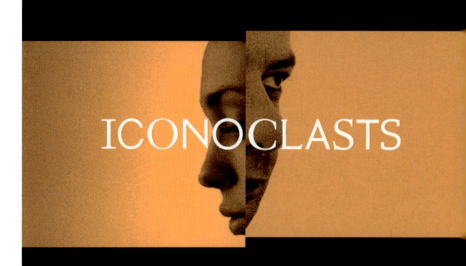

BD: Does the increasing specialization of TV content create new potentials and challenges for branding?

SUNDANCE CHANNEL: The niche channels provide great opportunities for crafting identities and personalities around a very singular and clear Channel positioning. It's exciting because you don't have to be all things to all people. It's about knowing your audience and delivering the content and the personality that's right for them.

BD: How does Sundance Channel see the future of the channel's design? Are there opportunities for development, or "just" the pure market pressure to update the brand periodically?

SUNDANCE CHANNEL: Sundance Channel is always evolving and the channel's design adapts and grows along with that. This past year we added an environmental night of programming called "The Green" to the channel. Not only did that provide a different kind of programming but it prompted us to explore new areas from a design perspective, notably the injection of illustration and – of course – the color green!

But there's also room for bolder elements – like the title sequence for "Iconoclasts" (this page and previous page).

... know that it takes me a while to be able to ...
... have to say in all fairness, I probably make 1 ...
... everything out, I probably make maybe eight ...
... that. Individual works. Not eight an edition.

TF
... So we're just now delivering the first one. So
there will probably be another.

GROUND

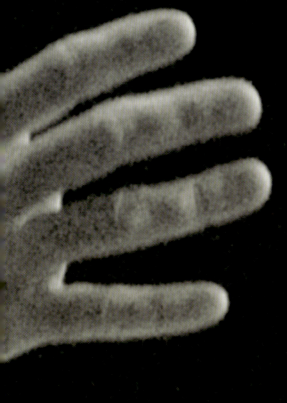

Both pages: opener "Big Ideas For A Small Planet".

big ido
FOR A SMALL PLANET

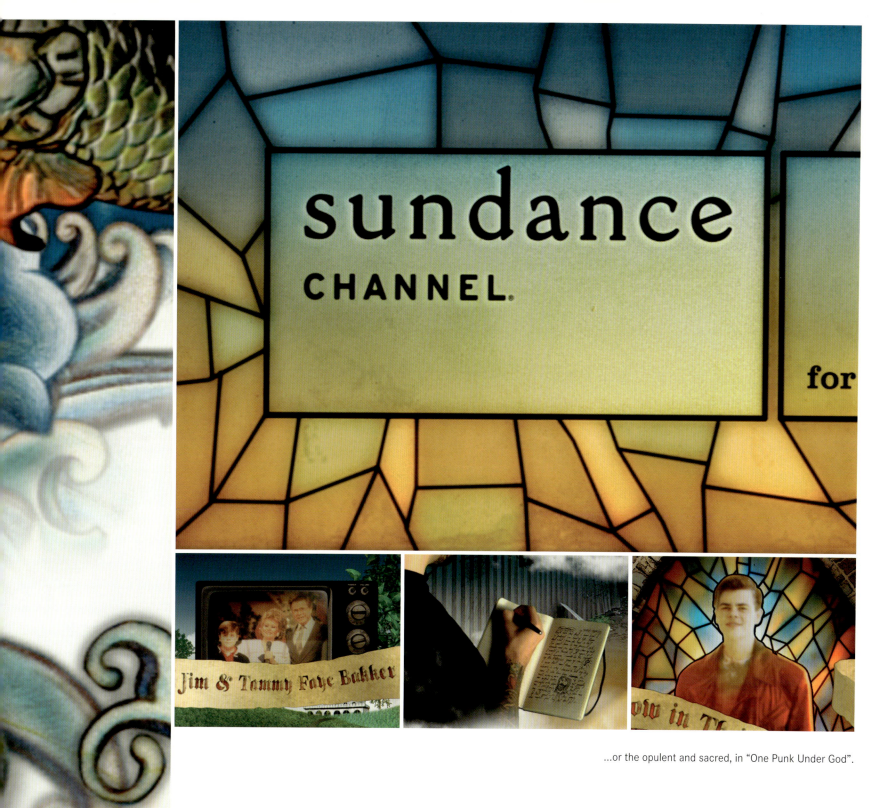

...or the opulent and sacred, in "One Punk Under God".

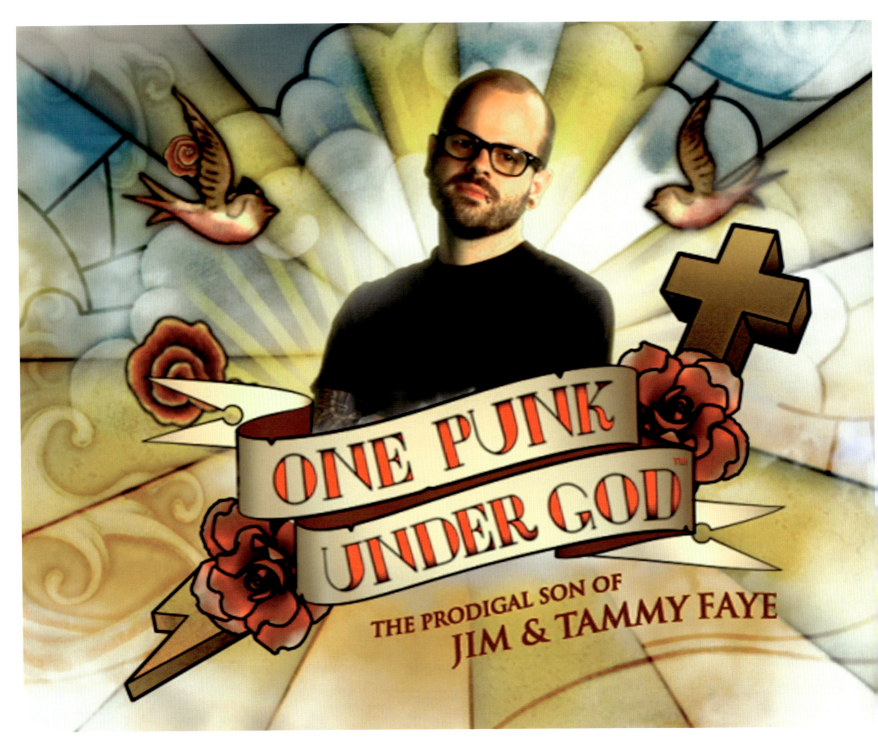

The "One Punk Under God" campaign on air (this page) and on billboards and posters (opposite page).

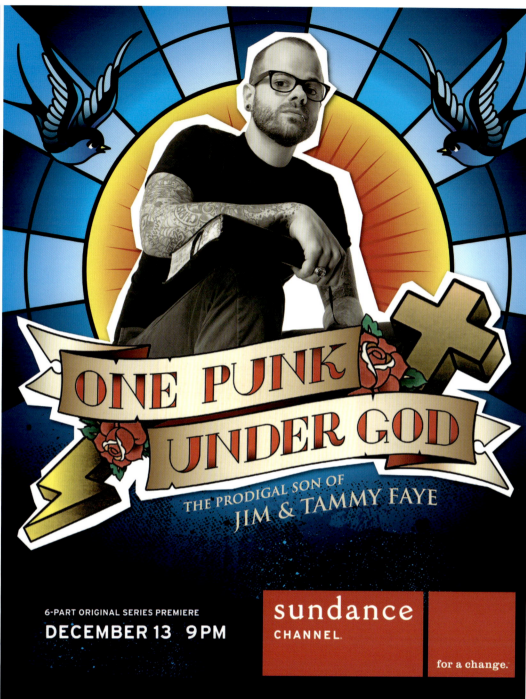

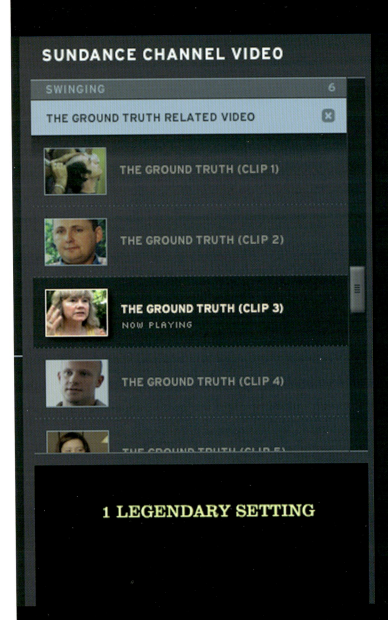

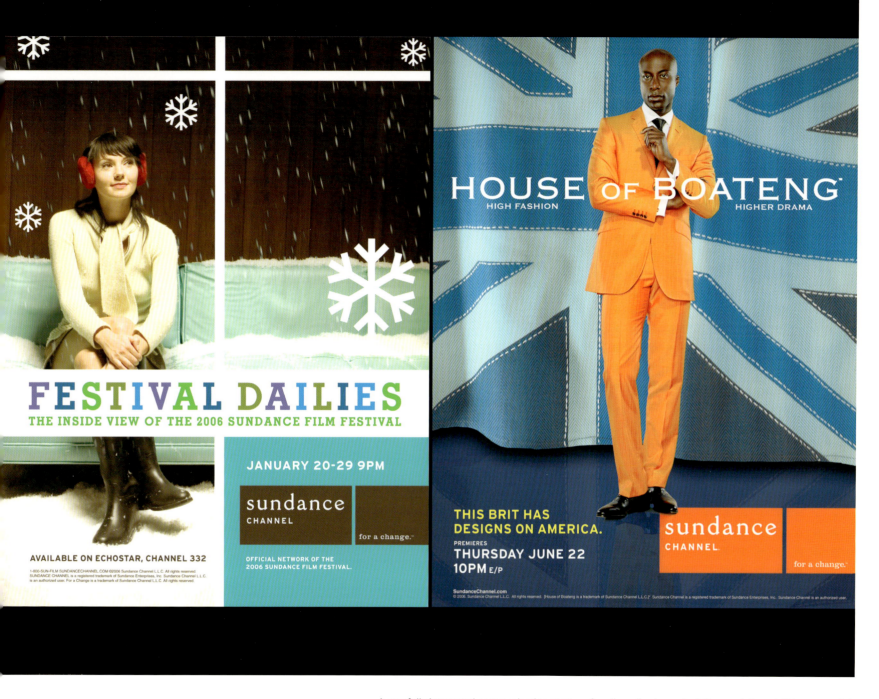

A carefully integrated communication strategy for all media channels: left page: internet, this page: print.

FOX cable network's FUEL TV / USA **FUEL TV**

The only rule governing the design universe of FOX cable network's FUEL TV is that there are no rules:
you just have to be innovative and cutting edge.
The mission is to tap into the latest trends and styles, or even set new ones...
Both pages from "RESPECT" SKATE ID by Brand New School.

Today's boys and young men are growing smarter, stronger, faster and more confident every day and they know it... They dream of the freedom that comes with adulthood, while wrapped in the security of their youth. They feel both tortured and empowered by their transition, and this duality governs their entire experience. Irreverent, fiercely loyal, and wary of strangers, they stand ready to challenge the establishment and are prepared for a revolution... Fueled by a voracious appetite for life, their wants and desires are many, yet this hunger is balanced by a sophisticated understanding of modern marketing that allows them to recognize a "sell-out" with ease. You only get one shot to prove your cool with them. If you blow it, they label you "lame" and banish you into oblivion. They are tuned in and turned on in ways their parents never imagined. In lives filled with emails, faxes, cell phones, video games, pagers and PDAs, all they know is the "digital" age. Their sisters and girlfriends get MTV, Pink, N'Sync and Carson Daly. But what do they get?

Team sports and band practice no longer satisfy their needs. These stimulus junkies turn to video games, music and ACTION SPORTS for diversion. But their tastes in gaming and music become fragmented quickly when genres of either are raised. Sports vs. Fantasy games, Rap vs. Techno, the splintering is endless. ACTION SPORTS (Skateboarding, Surfing, BMX, Freestyle Motocross, Snowboarding and Wakeboarding) are unlike any other influence on contemporary youth culture and have captured the imagination, energy and excitement of young men across the country and around the world.

Participants and enthusiasts are drawn to these activities not with the dream of becoming a professional, but for the chance to tap into a powerful and compelling experience that impacts every aspect of their lives. Regardless of which sport occupies their attention, they are drawn to it because it looks and is fun and carefree. It allows, in fact demands, individuality of expression. It offers camaraderie, language, clothes and ultimately a lifestyle that perfectly suits their needs...

FUEL TV is dedicated to this ideal. FUEL TV embraces the primal tenets of the teenage experience and celebrates the mysterious contradiction that is Youth Culture... From its name to its programming, from its logo to its graphics, from its promos and interstitials to its sound design, everything about FUEL TV is organic to action sports, an expression "of the culture", not "about it". In every aspect of its existence, FUEL TV speaks in an authentic voice, one that is fresh and new, yet vaguely familiar. It possesses the perspective of an insider who understands the nuances of the vital places, people, and events that define youth culture...

Where other networks have focused almost exclusively on competition, FUEL TV explores the depth and breadth of the action sports lifestyle, with an ever expanding offering of "free" action, interviews, profiles, news, travel, animation, entertainment, fashion, electronics, gaming and lots and lots and lots of music. Its programming is created by "best of breed" producers from throughout the global action sports industry, people who live and breath the culture everyday, and have unparalleled access to its most colorful characters.

FUEL TV is also about risk and opportunity, providing a testing ground for rising young talent, whether in front of the camera or behind. It discovers new riders, filmmakers, musicians, and artists who bring total commitment and endless passion to their endeavors. As such, it is an active force in action sports, leading and defining innovation, evolution and expression of youth culture.

The "reveal" ident (both sides) introduces some of the designers, illustrators and artists behind FUEL TV's design work. It's just a shame they are wearing masks... (Artists include Mike Giant, Chris Yormick, Dalek, Ben Woodward, Pose, and Axis).

The Vice President of Marketing and On-Air Promotions Jake Munsey, and the Senior Producer, On-Air Promotions, Todd Dever, both FUEL TV, kindly answered some questions about BROADCAST DESIGN (BD).

BD: Surfing, skateboarding and fun sports fuelled innovation in (print) design back in the 90s. Are they still providing exciting stimuli for audiovisual design in the new millennium?

JAKE MUNSEY: In short, yes. Take skateboarding, it draws individuals who want to do something different and it weeds out – through sheer difficulty and pain – the less committed. In essence you end up with, among other things, a small group of creative people who are sort of the youth counter culture today in America. Skateboarding and some of the other sports influence and are influenced by expressive individuals – it's a magnet for young independent thinkers and it's a place of opportunity for them too.

TODD DEVER: I'd say the influence of action sports on design started much earlier than the 90s. We saw how surfing had a big influence in the 60s and skateboarding in the 70s and 80s. The unique designs on skate decks were inspiring young artists to expand their creative expression from their riding to their artwork. Many of those designs infused punk rock elements with underground cartoons and fine art in a way that we still see today. Because your board is really a means of personal expression, it only makes sense that self-expression would inspire other art forms.

BD: Is there such a thing as typical East or West Coast design in the US TV world? Is there even such a thing as a specific American broadcast design?

JAKE MUNSEY: Of course. It's Westside gangster rap vs. Eastside old school hip hop.

Seriously, I'd like to think there's a difference. I'd hate for everything to just be a monoculture of which we only have different viewpoints. Certainly we can say there are different styles and themes associated with each coast, but a 'West Coast' style could easily be coming out of the east and vice versa. What I call a West Coast aesthetic tends to be characterized by youth subcultures like skateboarding and influenced by Pacific Rim nations. NYC, and the urban landscape there, I guess could be accepted as defining East Coast design. I've always lived around the Pacific though so I don't really know. Easily recognizable influences in the US design scene appear to be the graduate schools (Cal Arts, Art Center, RISD, Cranbrook, School of Visual Arts, Cooper Union, etc…) and specific design studios (ironically they're often bi-coastal).

TODD DEVER: Yeah whatever. Ditto… except it's north and south rather than east and west.

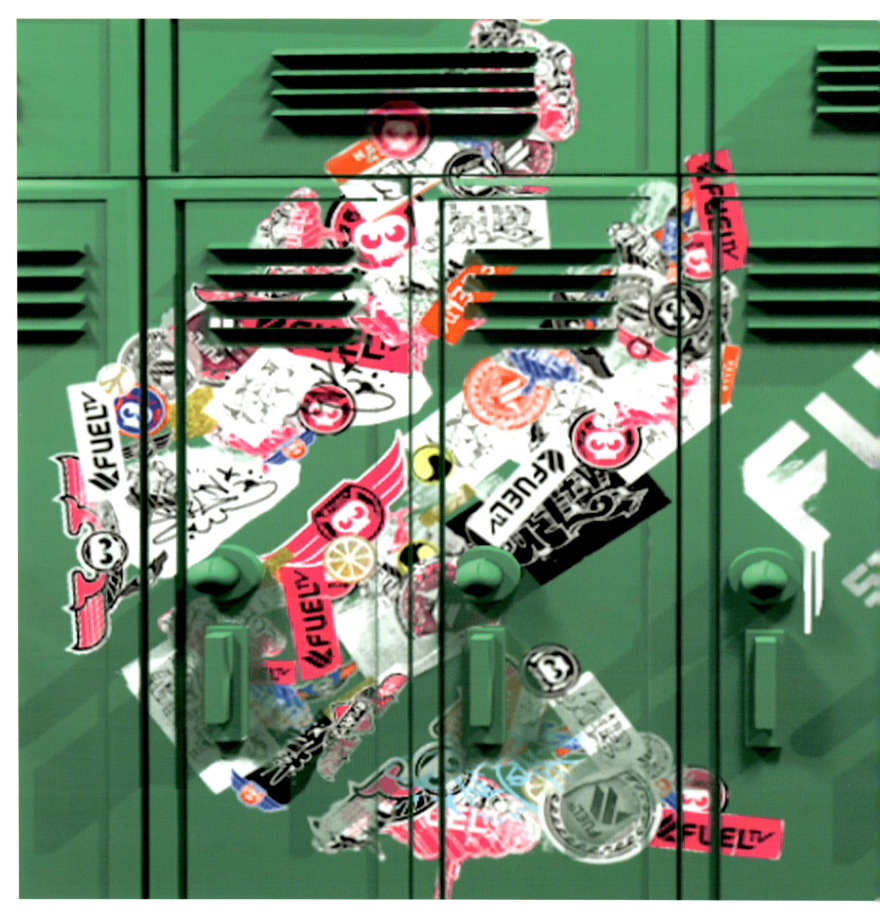

The FUEL TV logo can morph into the visual style chosen by the creator, thereby projecting the contextual concept of each piece onto the brand base itself – it becomes FUEL TV!

BD: A key theme for FUEL TV's audiovisual communication is variety. How do you manage to maintain a clear brand image?

TODD DEVER: I always imagine FUEL TV as an extension of the viewer's own environment. If you think about the bedroom of your typical teenager, you would probably see that it's full of all the stuff he loves – girls, skateboards, posters of bands, cartoons, art, girls, etc. I know my room was always full of the stuff I thought was cool. I didn't paint my room with a color scheme and only display what went with that theme. I surrounded myself with everything I thought was cool. While we do have a basic visual language to our broadcast design package, the idea of having a set theme or anything that smells like a marketing strategy is the kind of thing that turns our viewers off. Giving them a great experience is more important than giving them a consistent experience.

JAKE MUNSEY: First, we are passionate about the culture and are dedicated to being an authentic 'expression of it' rather than 'about it'. So the concrete form our brand takes visually, in motion and sound is derived from an essence and is more fluid or flexible than a set of characteristics and rules like a specific color pallet, etc... (Although we do at times choose to use certain constraints like having 'official' fonts.) Basically the consistency is derived from intellectual unity and the benefit is that the forms those ideas can take are almost unlimited.

In other words, the point is freedom of expression, to expect a progression of styles, to have the widest array of techniques and messages as possible within what would be accepted as true to skateboarding, surfing and the like.

BD: Another basic principle for the design seems to be the incorporation of a wide range of designers and studios. Which criteria do you use to select your partners and what (positive) effects come out of this variety?

TODD DEVER: Right from the beginning FUEL TV was conceived with great design in mind. Because several of our people on staff here come from a design background there was a real sense of excitement at the opportunity to work with the top design firms we could find. We are constantly on the lookout for great design work, whether it's coming from one of the wide roster of design firms we work with, or a new studio with a lot of creative talent. Of course we all have our favorite designers / studios because we know they will always come through with something amazing, but it's the ability to take the design somewhere special that really counts. While I appreciate the technical skills that go into making a great piece of animation, at the end of the day, it's really the creativity & storytelling that count. I don't care if it was the most complex 3D animation or created with a Popsicle stick, I'm looking for real inspiration.

Both pages from the Pinto series of IDs.
Produced by Brand New School.

When I look for new designers the first thing that catches my attention is something new and different that I haven't seen before. I may see it on their reel, on the web, even on YouTube. There is a lot of rehashing of old ideas on a lot of reels I see. Usually the first place I look on someone's website is not their latest reel, but for their experimental projects. That's where you find a lot of truly inspiring work and a good look at what the animators are really into.

JAKE MUNSEY: I started at FUEL TV right from the beginning – in fact I was the first person CJ Olivares (General Manager and the man with the vision) hired. I never really thought much about it, but right from the beginning I made choices that focused on bringing in different ideas, skills and viewpoints. For example, I worked with graphic designers from the print world to develop the logo and identity system, but hired the Brand New School creative team to develop the on-air look and promotional toolkit. Brand New School was perfect for the project because of their background, but also because they brought a team to the project that was pitching a wide variety of ideas at us. I really like the fact that we get to work with so many talented people – it's invigorating and the more talent we have contributing the better the channel gets. I just wish we had more resources to keep the volume of work up.

For criteria, I just don't let them hire anyone unless I like their work. Todd and I have similar tastes so it's never an issue or a source of disagreement... I think.

BD: What are the most important elements of the design? What's the philosophy behind FUEL TV's design?

TODD DEVER: When it comes to FUEL TV's on air look for promos and internally produced shows, my philosophy is keep it "fucked up". I want the look of the design and animation to have the feel that it was actually made by someone who watches the channel. What would I do if I were 17 years old and putting this together in my garage after school? Of course you bring your own sense of design and style to the table, but we like to keep things very raw. Before I started at FUEL TV I worked at several design studios and really had to figure out how to unlearn a lot of the things I would normally do to make something look "good". How would I approach this if I didn't have access to all the sophisticated software and plug-ins? It's always interesting when working with freelancers or outside companies to tell them "hey man, this is too good – I want it fucked up". And if I tell you your work is fucked up – take it as a compliment.

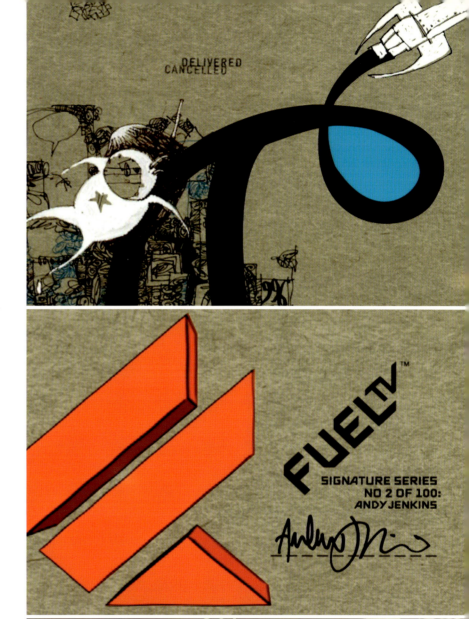

FUEL TV provides a platform for experimenting with all types of animation and new image generation techniques.
MTV held sway in that area in the 80s and 90s.
Both pages: "Chris Pastras Signature ID #8". Produced by Brand New School.

JAKE MUNSEY: Using hand drawn, textural and raw elements are pervasive FUEL TV themes and they're a nice counterweight to the sophisticated channel IDs. I think it's really the use of those two together (seemingly contradicting each other) in a unified way that makes our channel stand out.

The foundation, created at Brand New School, includes the aforementioned hand-drawn patterns, the buttons (i.e., pins), typography, paint drips and the first ten IDs (where the variety of styles, ideas and techniques are clearly demonstrated). Another important principle is to use signifiers or references to counter cultural movements or themes that were subversive (or rebellious) in their respective day. Which seems like an obvious choice, but Jens Gehlhaar really clarified this philosophy in a way that took it out of the realm of just 'raw and edgy' (said with sarcasm) and made the thinking, references and allusions intelligent. Because of this clarity every talented and intelligent person who has worked on the brand has had a framework to make smart decisions about what is germane to FUEL TV and what isn't.

BD: From the point of view of a channel, which serves a very specific audience, would you say that the channel's audiovisual style makes it possible to reach the audience in a simpler, clearer way? (And there are lots of very sensitive subgroups here too?)

TODD DEVER: If you really look at our audience, you have several subgroups such as skater, surfers, freestyle moto fans etc. Each sport really has its own culture and visual language. Yes there are overlaps, but surfers and freestyle moto riders don't generally aspire to the same visual aesthetic. So, in a way we don't cater to the sport specific cultures as much as try to create an environment where they can all coexist. Just because one segment of the audience identifies with a certain sport, doesn't mean they're not out doing the other sports on the weekend. It's really all about individual freedom of expression and if we get that idea across then we've succeeded. One way we know we've done it is by the loyalty of our viewers. So many turn on FUEL TV and leave it on all day.

JAKE MUNSEY: We have a niche audience that is incredibly diverse in age, nationality, creed, income, interests and values. The visual language, through abstraction and the use of universal ideas, engages our audience while avoiding the pitfalls of the lowest common denominator approach.

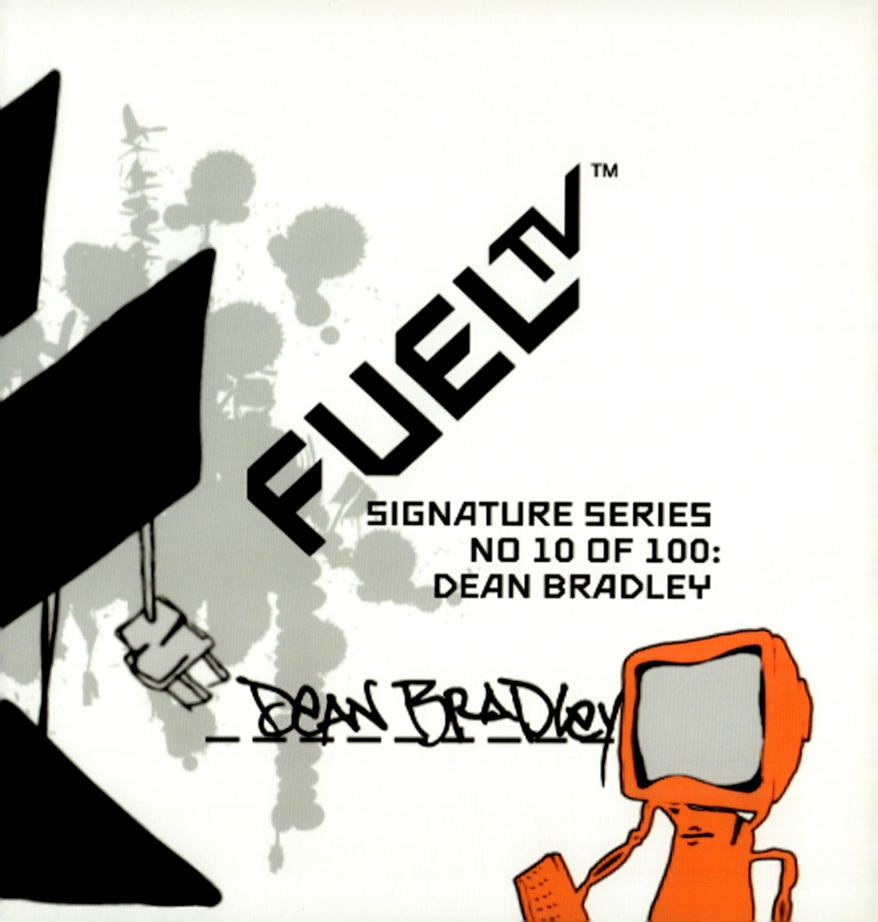

FUEL™

SIGNATURE SERIES
NO 10 OF 100:
DEAN BRADLEY

With the signature series 100, designers and design shops will feature the FUEL TV brand using their specific approach. This involves signature boards on the skater scene... Both pages from the "Dean Bradley" signature series #10, produced by Todd Dever.

BD: What's the X of 100 Signature Series? What's it all about?

JAKE MUNSEY: It's the Signature Series. Todd can explain the idea. It became a series when I looked at the original pitch from BNS and said this should be a series of IDs. They asked how many and I just picked a round number that sounded good... one hundred.

TODD DEVER: These IDs were inspired by the idea of signature skateboard decks created by or for athletes, and serve many purposes: to associate the channel with a well-known athlete, to introduce an exciting and appropriate artist to the audience, or to serve as a new and exciting outlet for athletes who express themselves in art or music. The only consistent element in all these IDs is the end card, which features a massive FUEL TV logo as well a line of type that is used to title or to tag the piece.

We have featured artists from many different mediums from film (Doug Aitken) to performance art (Jason Irwin) to illustrators, painters and cartoonists. Many of these artists have never had the opportunity to see their work move and it's always an interesting challenge to create something that is true to their vision and style.

BD: As we saw in Episode 17 of the Signature Series (Stardust's Cardboard Robot), street culture (spraying, tagging etc.) plays an important role in the look and feel of the channel. At FUEL TV, do you see that as a kind of cultural activity? (Seeing as how most of the current music TV stations have given up on that role!)

TODD DEVER: Street culture is something that has been a part of FUEL TV from day one. It really reflects much of the DIY attitude that has been a part of youth culture from the punk rock scene of the 70s. While there has always been that tagging aspect of street art, it really has a much more creative side to it too. There are really amazing pieces of art being put up all around us. Once you get beyond the basic graffiti tags (which have a big influence on typography) you see lots of great work being done with posters, stickers... all kinds of things. Street artists are always pushing the boundaries of style, technique and even technology that eventually works its way into more "sophisticated" mediums like TV. Because anyone can afford to do it you find it's often where the up and coming artists turn to first with their most personal and inspired work.

The techniques used for station idents also feature live action.
Both pages by Jason Irwin, from the signature series.
Overleaf: "cardboard robot" by Stardust, from the signature series.

340

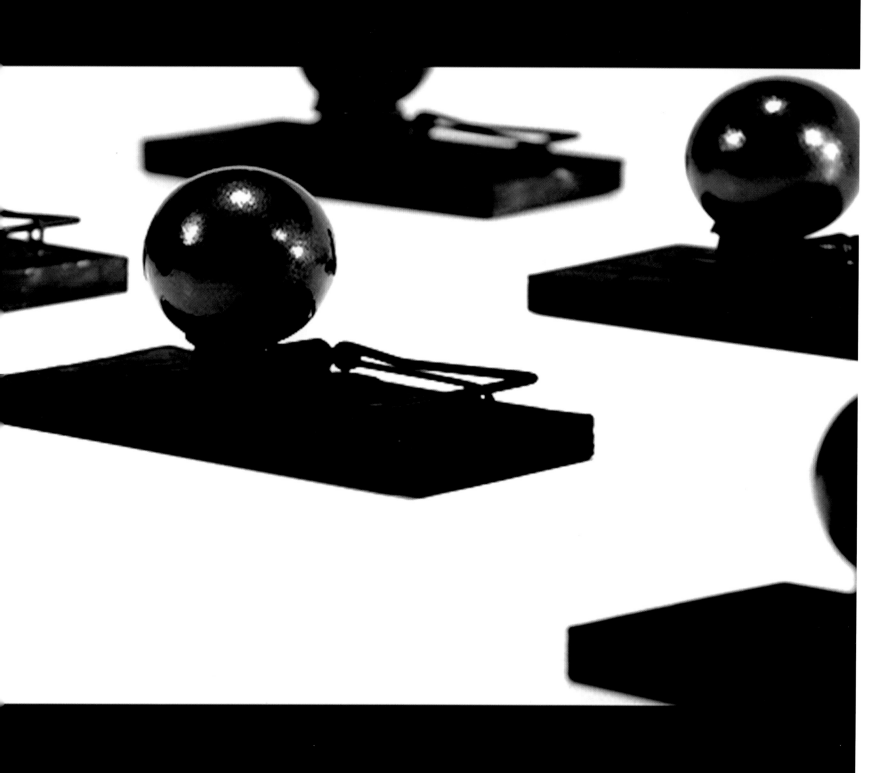

The Cardboard Robot signature series ID was based on an experimental film idea by the guys at Cardboard Robot. It was about the excessive age of technology and the individual's increasing ability to segregate from the idea that we may all be a very integral part of nature. In our ID the robot is pasting up a wheat paste poster and then enters into the world of the poster, ultimately tearing it down to reveal the FUEL TV logo. Part of the message here is that the artwork is a living entity, which is a wonderful thing about street art. Once the piece of art is put out there it really takes on a life of its own.

JAKE MUNSEY: It's pretty common in America for whites to co-opt black culture (e.g., rock n' roll, blues, break dancing, speech and art). We focus on the youth culture and lifestyle around skateboarding, surfing and whatnot. That focus is broader and more inclusive of divergent ideas that what you see coming from other American channels. Again our goal is to be an authentic expression of the culture – not about it. Today you see a lot of aspiring artists drawn to this because it's just cool. Once they start they usually end up putting in time as graf writers to build their reputation and credibility. I think the longevity of graffiti, stenciling, wheat pasting and the like speak to its appeal and strength. Besides it's rebellious and expressive. And you can't beat the fumes (just kidding).

BD: In the independent world (which accounts for a major part of your target audience?), it's particularly important to be at the cutting edge when it comes to using (audio)visual codes. How do you do that? Do you think you manage to create trends yourselves occasionally?

TODD DEVER: Jake is much more cutting edge than I am. I'm only cutting edge on Tuesdays. How does one try to be cutting edge? I just go for what ever excites me. To set out to be cutting edge seems like an odd way to go at it. As far as setting trends goes, I save that for Thursdays. I'm cooking up a really good trend right now.

JAKE MUNSEY: We create trends in so far as we allow trend setting artists a chance to do something their more conservative clients won't. I think we have been a strong influence because when we allow something to happen it legitimizes the approach and makes it easier for others to pursue their more innovative ideas. It also works in reverse for us to. Ironically, because we're a small channel you'll rarely find someone who believes we started something because they're more likely to see it played out on MTV or a Burger King commercial. And the reality is that these ideas are coming from so many different creative teams (e.g., BNS, Freestyle Collective, Shilo, Stardust, Natl TV, etc...) and we really play a smaller part in it. Sometimes I feel more like a curator than a creative director.

BD: The Internet platform plays a very important role for FUEL TV. How closely linked is the planning of on-air and online?

TODD DEVER: The internet plays a more and more important role in connecting viewers with the channel. While we've always had to plan things with web content in mind, things are getting more and more connected. I think we are moving away from seeing our web presence as a place to go to get information about FUEL TV to a place where our viewers can connect with it and other viewers. Our web presence is becoming more and more interactive and it's now a great place for users to become a part of the FUEL TV experience. We go so far as to having our users creating content that we use on the air. These guys (and girls) are pretty fanatical with their love for the channel. While we are a small channel and have an even smaller web staff, we are trying to pull the audience in to help us promote the programming that they feel so passionate about.

JAKE MUNSEY: I'm responsible for our marketing, on-air promotions, creative services, research, public relations, advertising and our website. I'd like to think they're unified, but I'm so close to all these areas now that I tend to see the flaws more than the successes. It's really hard to have different creative teams in very different mediums stay in alignment when you're preaching expressive freedom and visual progression. When we're struggling I just tell everyone to follow the on-air look, but when we're in the flow everyone and everything is collaborating and it's all perfection.

BD: FUEL TV is also available as a podcast. What implication does that have in terms of the design elements you use and the control of your brand?

TODD DEVER: All of the new podcast / online / mobile phone mediums each pose a challenge. It seems like once you've decided how you're going to deal with one thing, something new pops up. It's really an interesting time in our industry. On one hand it's exciting to be part of all these new delivery mediums, on the other hand we know that half of them will not be around in a couple years so we try to target the ones we think are worthwhile and put our efforts into customizing for those platforms. Of course you need to take into consideration type size and aspect ratio when dealing with the small screen, but we've had to develop a series of mobile phone targeted logo tags to make sure the audience gets the mesage.

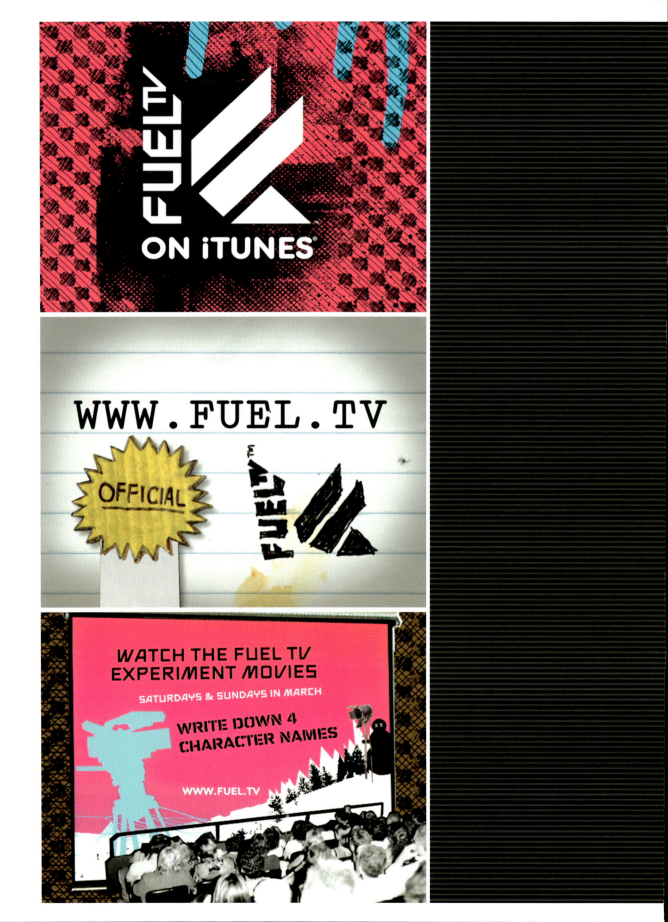

JAKE MUNSEY: The podcasts and electronic sell through of shows makes me nervous because we lose control over a lot of the framing (i.e., context and packaging). Still it holds promise and I look forward to when we are able to be more experimental with that distribution channel.

What I'm most interested in right now are tools and platforms that democratize the creative and technology. So we're exploring the Open ID system, microformats for content, user generated content, mash-ups and open source projects. The possibilities that exist when you move from atoms to bytes are incredible and we should be looking at our work as systems (dynamic not static or controlling) now more than ever.

BD: How does FUEL TV see the future, in terms of the shifts in distribution paths? Would an IP-based program delivery, for example, increase the potential audience? What effects would that have on design and branding?

TODD DEVER: Ok Jake this is your world. Sounds to me like we're going to have to buy a whole bunch of new equipment... Again!

JAKE MUNSEY: The audience grows, as more people are aware of and able to get our content. The actual available audience – people interested in this subject – will probably not grow that dramatically. How much time our audience spends interacting with our content will grow more and more, but there's a limit to how much attention and time someone has. I don't think it's about a larger audience, but a more empowered audience. What will change is our practice of design and branding and its value to us.

Number 12 in the signature series.
Both pages from "dalek". Produced by Ka-Chew.

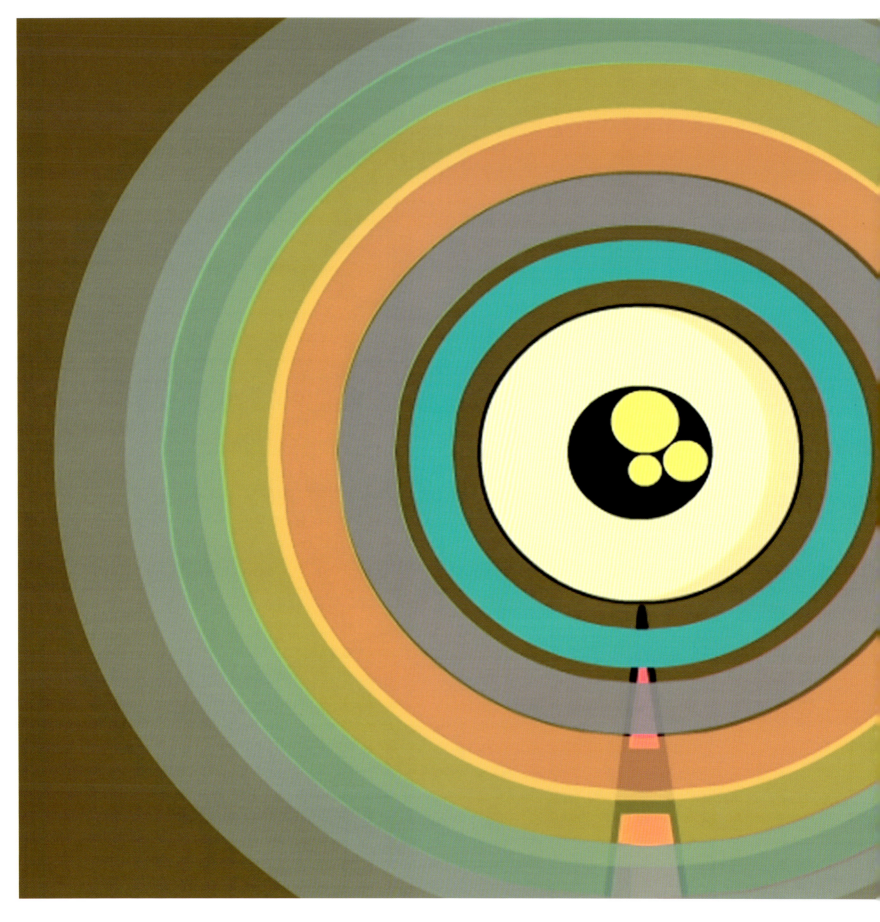

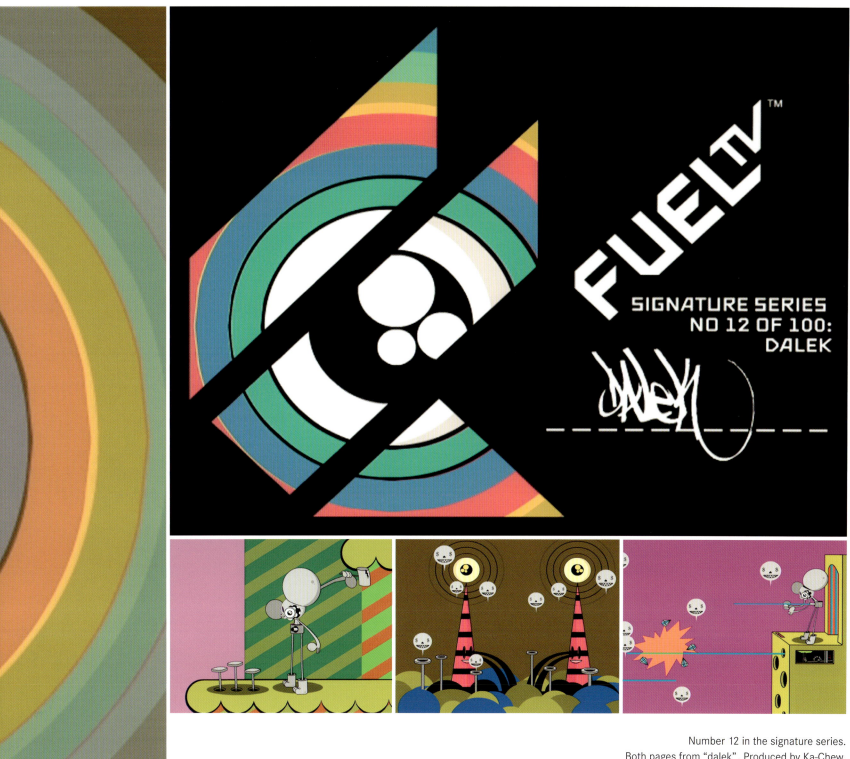

Number 12 in the signature series.
Both pages from "dalek". Produced by Ka-Chew.

Visual work for FUEL TV is seamlessly transformed into print design.

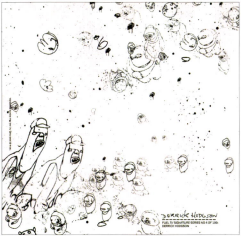

FUEL TV SIGNATURE SERIES NO 10 OF 100:
DEAN BRADLEY

ARD and ZDF's Children's Channel / Germany **KI.KA**

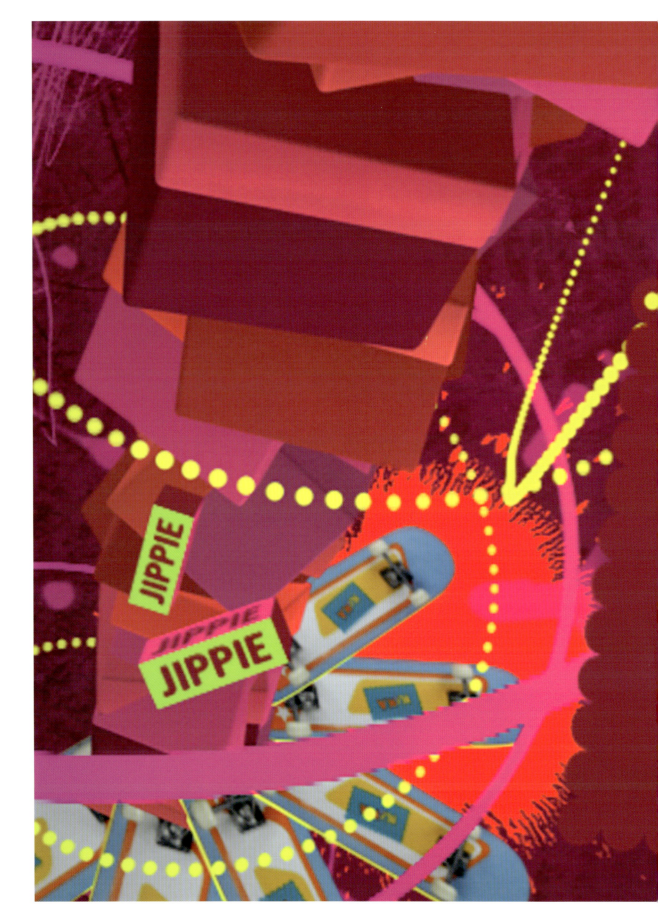

356

KI✗KA

VON ARD UND ZDF

KI.KA is a public television channel for young viewers aged between three and thirteen. A joint venture of ARD (a consortium of Germany's federal public service broadcasters) and ZDF, it has been broadcasting since January 1st, 1997.

The influence of the media on children's daily lives continues to grow, and television remains the primary medium for this. A TV channel especially for children should not and can not assume the role of a parent, but it can provide food for thought. With a variety of programmes, the children's channel of ARD and ZDF encourages and supports the social, emotional and cognitive development of its young audience.

The public service children's channel should inform, educate, advise and entertain and in doing so, meet the specific needs of the young target audience. KI.KA (from the German KinderKanal, "children's channel") thus makes an invaluable contribution towards preparing its viewers for the demands of the future. It imparts knowledge in a variety of ways and is the only channel to broadcast up-to-date information on a daily basis. The channel deals with themes in a way that is suitable for children in children's news programmes, magazine slots, interactive live shows, advice shows and also in documentaries, fiction and entertainment formats.

KI.KA's programming offers something for children at different developmental stages and from all social backgrounds. The channel's designers are particularly careful when creating programmes for very young children – programmes for this age group demand highly responsible attitudes and awareness of educational and developmental issues. Thanks to the mutual efforts of ARD and ZDF, KI.KA has the best produced preschool formats in Germany.

The channel is obviously advert-free. KI.KA encourages self-confidence, not brand awareness, and promotes positive values, not products.

KI.KA never loses sight of the fact that children live in a social reality which is constantly changing and is not conflict-free. Children's TV is not 'happy family' TV and has a duty to depict the realities of children's lives. It also has to provide positive ways of dealing with conflict. The theme of violence is not ignored, but violence is never depicted as a way of solving problems, or used merely in order to build tension.

KI.KA is the first port of call for children and is always there for them. It's a sounding board for the opinions of children and represents their interests. Because: ARD and ZDF's children's channel is on children's side and at children's side.

VORSCHULKIN

SCHULKIND

PRETEEN

The colour schemes for the different age groups (preschool, primary school and preteens)...

The Head of Promotion & Design of KI.KA, Ellen Kärcher, and the Art Director of FEEDMEE, Alexandra Grundmann, (> p. 392), kindly answered some questions about BROADCAST DESIGN (BD).

BD: Children's TV is of course a deeply ideological affair...(?)
KI.KA: Ideology sounds too political, too hard. That kind of approach is more what you'd expect from an educational channel, and KI.KA doesn't see itself that way. We see ourselves as more of an general interest channel aimed at children and younger viewers.

BD: Can you say what those values related to the design are?
FEEDMEE: The look is based on collage. There's a combination of elements which are specific to the target age groups and are laid out in advance, and objects from the children's daily lives. Saying "daily lives", we felt that it was important to use unusual objects like washing up brushes or garden hoses as well – not just familiar playroom stuff – partly to stimulate the children's imagination by surprising them, and partly to set a cheerful new trend that goes against kitschy teddy bear design.
KI.KA: In this world we only show things which are totally free of violence and have a certain 'value'. This is an issue that reflects the channel's principle aim of meeting the needs of children as viewers. The target audience of "children" is divided into target audience subgroups, so KI.KA divides the programmes and their packaging into individual clusters which reflect the different developmental stages of the different age groups. For formats that are aimed at toddlers, for example, we use objects that you would find in their playrooms. We select soft, cuddly, tactile things which are meant to encourage the children to touch them and play...

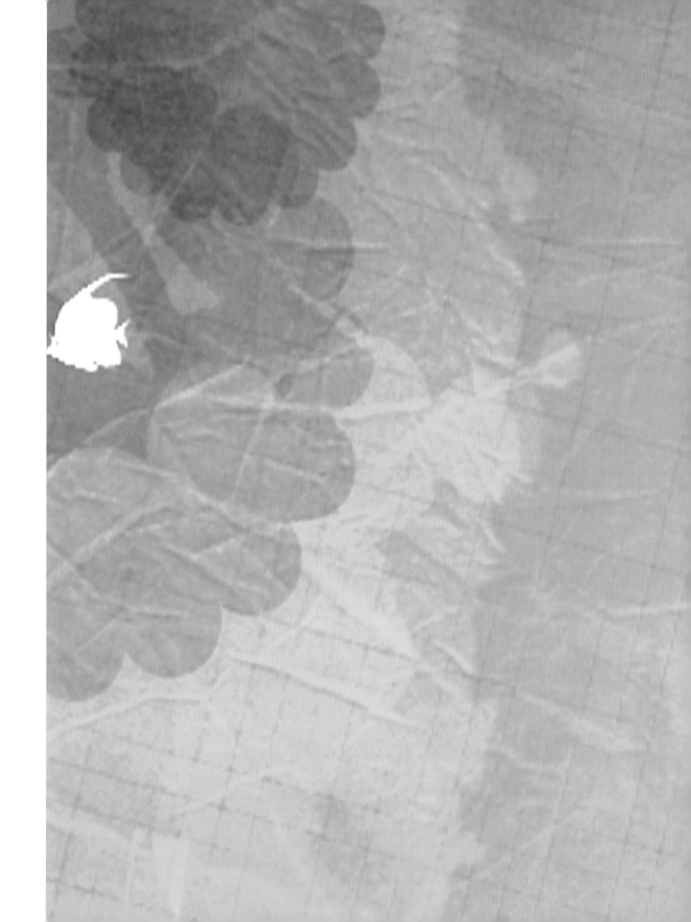

C
B
A

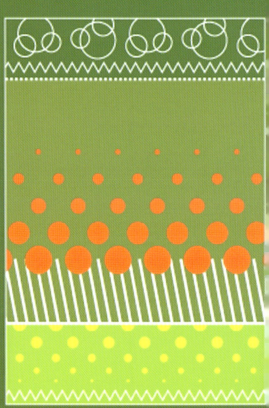

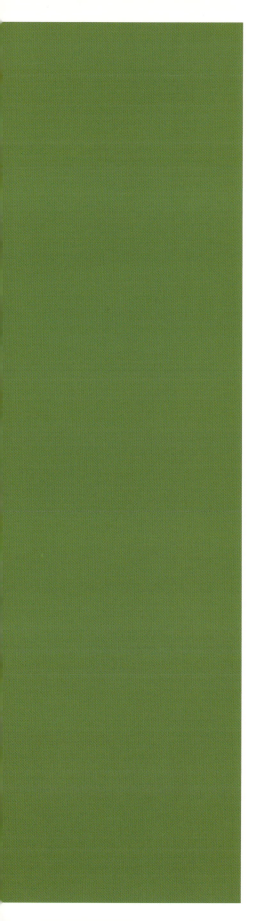

Visualisation from feedmee's pitch presentation.
The rapid pace at which children develop makes them an extremely diverse target audience.

BD: Clustering the age-specific target audience subgroups is a big challenge. How do you go about it?

FEEDMEE: In the brief, KI.KA divides its viewers into three main groups: pre-school, school age and pre-teens. This is correspondingly reflected in the design, starting with three different colour schemes (sunny yellow and light for pre-school, blue for school-age and bright pink for the pre-teens). The starting point for the channel's look was the idea that children grow up with the channel and are kind of accompanied on an evolutionary process through different stages of childhood (sic!). The visual radius, the complexity, grow along with the young viewers' attentions spans.

BD: Does knowledge about children's perceptive abilities play a role in that kind of design process?

KI.KA: This is where KI.KA's competence comes in – this is our core business and we know what we're talking about. We provide our agency / agencies with very detailed briefs which are obviously informed by our know-how. The channel also works with universities who have an established expertise in our field, for example with the Institute for Communication and Media Studies at Leipzig University, Professor Schorb, or with Dr. Maya Götz at the IZI in Munich.

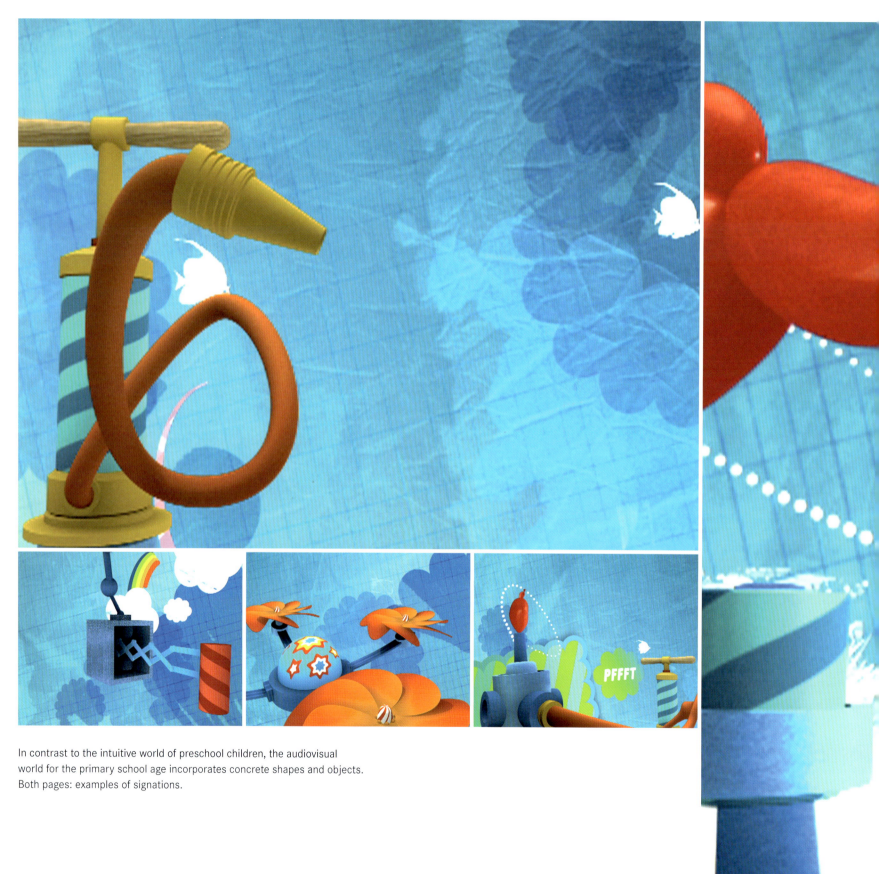

In contrast to the intuitive world of preschool children, the audiovisual
world for the primary school age incorporates concrete shapes and objects.
Both pages: examples of signations.

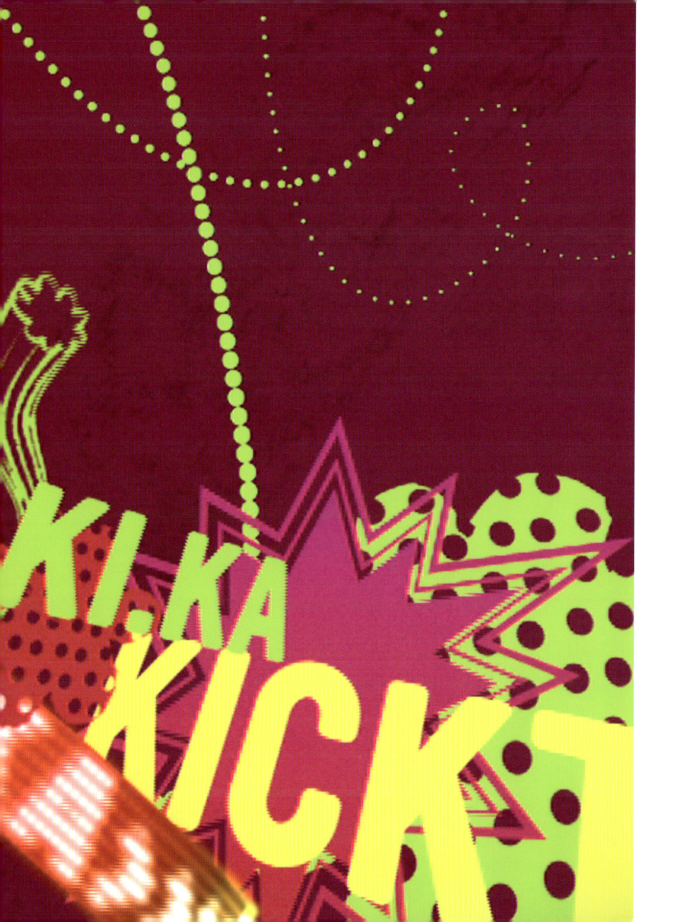

BD: How would you judge the design in terms of the channel's status as a PSB?

KI.KA: In principle, we don't see ourselves, as a PSB, as different to our private competitors. We have to position ourselves in a plural free TV market just the same as other channels do (in this context, I'd leave out the whole "the finance behind all of this is not important" stuff – obviously it's not that simple, but I think it's not that relevant here) – every channel wants to be unique.

BD: Does the lead agency see that differently? (particularly as it has so many projects for commercial channels?)

FEEDMEE: Definitely! At the end of the day, a channel is defined by its content and at KI.KA you see a very different way of going about things, and the standard of quality that's demanded. Compared to profit-driven channels, there are clear differences, which from the broadcasters' perspectives can hardly be avoided. The channel's aim – to make relevant television for children – is obviously reflected in the design criteria. Of course the channel should be distinctive, but there are limits!

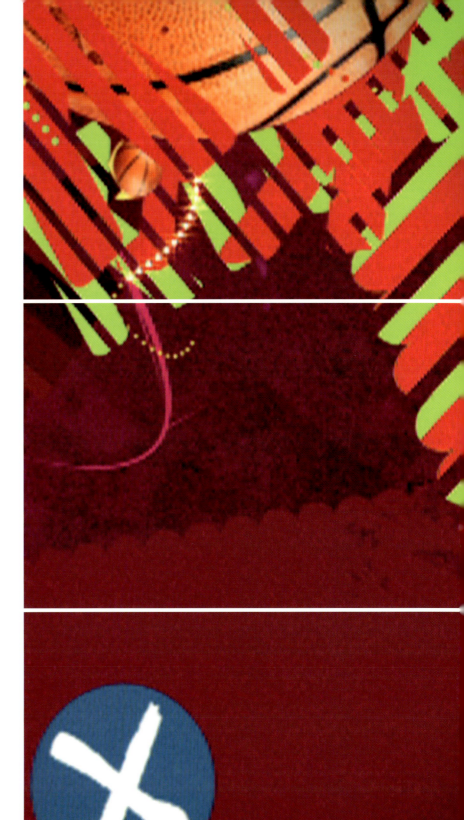

HEUTE

FREITAG 8:05
Bernd's Hitparade

DIENSTAG 12:30
Sindbad

DONNERSTAG 20:15
The Tribe

EINE SENDUNG IM

KI.KA

VON ARD UND ZDF

WWW.KIKA.DE

KI.KA's On-Air promotion is aimed at parents as much as the children.
Both pages: KI.KA's On-Air promotion.
Page 372: examples of trailers (left: trailer opener for programmes aimed at the 6-9 age group;
right: info screens for all three target age groups)
Page 373: KI.KA closedown / copyright board.

BD: What are the basis parameters for the design of the umbrella brand?

KI.KA: That was a redesign - the most important elements, like the logography and its colours, were to be kept. The viewers recognise these things and that's really valuable. Studies have shown that even pre-reading age children are able to identify our brand by its logo. Another basic principle is the division of the audience into three target groups, as we've already discussed, which enables us to use different modes of address.

BD: Did the corporations [ARD and ZDF, the first and second German TV channels] play a deciding role in the channel's design?

KI.KA: As is standard in the industry, we pitched to find the right agency for our redesign. Then we went to the programme's commissioners with the results and argued the case for the idea we liked best. We persuaded ARD and ZDF's representatives, so now we have a design which we can support without any compromises.

The design used to address the preteen target group is considerably more complex.
The concept of association is introduced, using the children's ability to reflect on what they're seeing.
Both pages: examples of trailer packaging.

BD: In terms of the packaging of individual formats, there's always a dilemma between keeping a programme's individual character on the one hand, and generating a fixed channel identity on the other. How do you deal with that?

FEEDMEE: We'd thought about that conflict when we were developing the design. The collage principle gives you a certain openness and flexibility on the one hand, and on the other, the specific characteristics of the elements creates a very clear basis. This is reflected in the packaging of individual formats, where we combined predetermined CI / collage elements with pieces which were transplanted from the individual programme. This lets you bring together target audience subgroups, brand and content in a very natural way.

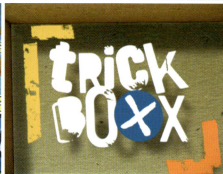

KI.KA uses a wide range of animation and image techniques. This means that there are always fresh elements in the design.
This page: format packaging for "musicboxx" and "trickboxx"; opposite page: "trickboxx kino".

BD: The "Mitmachmühle" format[1] is a good example of how corporate branding and individual design can work together. How were the individual elements developed?

KI.KA: As the name suggests, this is a programme which is meant to get children involved in a very interactive way, both directly, in the context of the programme, as well as via the internet. Because the core audience here is toddlers, elements of the "pre-school" design were used to generate a complete 3D world, which is echoed in the animation and especially in the studio design. The expansion into the 3D world proved worked very smoothly – because the core CD (and here I do mean corporate design, "identity" means a lot more) is of course two dimensional and not (obviously) suited to 3D animation.

It was also important to make sure that the young viewers always knew they were watching a KI.KA format, and we accomplished that really well. Feedback from the children showed that they didn't have any problems recognising that this design was a KI.KA design, and they picked it up in the set design too.

FEEDMEE: There's a high creative consistency which is achieved primarily through the bold design vocabulary, which includes things like simple outlines for objects, the colour scheme which was chosen and the relaxed tempo of the narration. This basic nature of the elements clearly references the brand and the target audience subgroups.

KI.KA: That format also proved that the design principles mean that other designers can work in the KI.KA look too, because FEEDMEE didn't do the "Mitmachmühle", and the quality is higher than you might expect. Last but not least, the quality of the process is emphasised by all the children's pictures and art work that they send us every day. That's really important feedback for us and says a lot about how well the individual elements are accepted.

BD: What are the demands for promotion in children's TV?

KI.KA: Again, we divide everything into three groups, reflecting the children's different attention spans. For example, the pre-school mode of address uses very little text and it's slower than say the pre-teen stuff, where we do play about with action and humour in the trailers – more than with irony – KI.KA's head of programme doesn't like irony much. The most important thing for us is to get the "what and when" across – the children have to receive clear information.

We also like freestanding trailers, that is to say that apart from the KI.KA corner bug, there's no constant graphic identification – at the end, all the important information is summarised again on a final slate. Also in terms of programming, trailers are generally allocated to an age group and shown until the end of the segment for that age group. Then we start showing the trailers for the next target group cluster. So using the idea of the channel growing with the children, this approach gives children the chance to access a higher age group and the content that's specific to that group. We're also aiming at an audience flow.

1 "Mit-Mach-Mühle", literally "Get-Involved-Mill", is an arts and crafts programme with a high level of input from children.

Opposite page: set design for [the art programme] MitMachMühle and examples from the on air promotion.
Page 384, left: MitMachMühle's set.
Right and page 385: Designs for KI.KA's film series "Lollywood".

BD: The interlocking of on-air and off-air elements obviously plays a major role in children's TV. How important is it in the design conception?

KI.KA: This summer, there's going to be a series of open air events for children again. Entire town squares will be transformed into a KI.KA world, using the familiar on-air design elements...

FEEDMEE: When we were developing the design, we had TV designers working with print people, onliners, sound designers and so on. Today, it's standard in the industry that all media channels need to be fully operationally integrated.

KI.KA: We see the internet as a particularly important secondary medium, the KI.KA site has an enormous number of hits... (We're also experimenting with mixing on air and online forms). With an online presence, you obviously need to take the non-linear nature of the medium into account, so we use a mixed media approach online, i.e., on our site the designs and colours for the different age groups often appear next to each other. And that shows a further strength of the corporate design: the different target group designs, which are individually very different, work brilliantly together. There's definitely a great future for hybrid forms and also offer new possibilities for branding (e.g. "Heldenmacher"); we proved that with our "Heldenmacher clips" for the "Platz für Helden" format[2]. Children could use the internet tools provided to tell us about their own personal heroes – and then they were shown on air.

2 "Heldenmacher" ("Hero Makers") was a show where groups of children had ten days to complete major challenges to benefit their local communities, like building a circus ring from scratch. The children were then rewarded by being named heroes. A website called "Platz für Helden" ("A Place for Heroes") was set up to accompany the series.

The brand is also consistently applied to merchandising (this page) and print (next page).

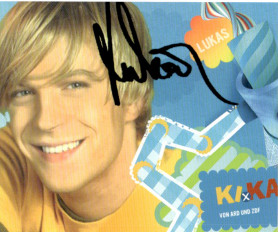

FILMLEUTE GESUCHT!

Kino macht Spaß! Aber Filme selber machen noch viel mehr! Alles, was Du dazu wissen musst, erfährst Du im Internet unter www.trickboxx.de oder im KI.KA –

jeden Sonntag um 11:15 Uhr

Opposite page, left: KI.KA print.
In addition to the broadcast channel, KI.KA's website (opposite page, right) is an important platform
for the broadcaster, providing the chance to experiment with bringing different media formats together.
This page: still from the "Lollywood" series opener.

FEEDMEE DESIGN GMBH

ADRESS   Lichtstrasse 43 a
            50825 Cologne, Germany

PHONE   +49 221 546 76 0
FAX   +49 221 546 76 10

CONTACT   Kerstin Kohle
            kerstin@feedmee.de
            www.feedmee.de

"Because we're hungry!" This is the simple answer to the commonly posed question as to why FEEDMEE is called FEEDMEE. They are incredibly hungry for new ideas and their realization, and for participating in the visible world. This design agency team constantly thirsts for action – and is far from becoming sated.

FEEDMEE's bill of fare is highly diverse: The graphic artists, art directors and concept designers on their team are creative in all related fields – from classic broadcasting and media design to the development of entirely new TV formats and characters, film and video headers and credits, video installations, image campaigns as well as designs for the print media.

Their ravenous appetite began in 1999 when Susanne Lüchtrath, Gerhard Menschik und Anton Riedel got together and founded FEEDMEE in Cologne. These three directors of the design agency – each one with many years of experience in the field of TV design – set the ball rolling. This ball has in the meantime passed many noteworthy milestones – most recently (2004) the Eyes & Ears special prize "Innovation" and the BDA gold ribbon in the category of Best Broadcast Design On-Air for the Playhouse Disney station design – and is currently moving at full speed.

Despite insatiable hunger, the Lüchtrath, Menschik, Riedel trio is always concerned with balancing their diet. As a result, the design agency has never been limited in the scope of its activities. It boils its soup in the caldrons of children's television and the music channels; it feeds from the bowls of the private as well as public television sectors; it cherishes German and international cuisine alike. Currently, FEEDMEE is involved in providing fodder for twelve hungry mouths, but depending on the status of current jobs, it invites additional regular guests to table. This interdependence with specialists from all walks of life guarantees the influx of innovative ideas and the continuous opportunity to experiment with the unknown. Repeatedly looking beyond the edge of your own bowl is FEEDMEE's special recipe. But always with a growling stomach.

Björn Bartholdy studied communication design at Merzakademie Stuttgart / Germany, and media design at the Academy of Media Arts in Cologne / Germany. In addition he freelanced as a TV designer for Bayerischer Rundfunk, RTL, VOX and VIVA. Later Björn Bartholdy founded "cutup", agency for media design and worked for the company as a managing director and creative director for a decade. The agency (major shareholder was Bertelsmann frome 1999) was awarded various national and international prices in the fields of film and television design and new media. In parallel he supervised the department "Virtual Design" at Film Academy Baden-Württemberg, Ludwigsburg, and for many years he was board member of "Eyes and Ears of Europe", the European association for design, promotion and marketing of audiovisual media. Since 2003 Björn Bartholdy has been responsible for the department "audiovisual media" at Köln International School of Design.

www.bmpltd.de
www.kisd.de

GLOSSAR

Brand: a term used internationally to refer to all of the elements that make up a product or service, such as name, logo, design, claim, and so on. These various components create a meta-image of a public organisation or corporation: the brand.

(Brand, Station)-Ident: short animation or live action clips (or combinations of the two), that promote the channel brand.

(Generic, Format)-Opener: format opening sequence. A short piece of animation or live action (or combinations of the two), that brands the specific format of a channel.

Teaser: a short clip that promotes a specific programme (for example a teaser trailer as part of on-air promotion) or event on a TV channel.

(Channel)-Programming: in the context of television, the term "programming" refers to the specific set of formats and their layout on the channel's timeline.

On-Air & Off-Air Design: When television is broadcast "on-air", the main design features of a TV channel are shown on screen – this is called "On-Air Design". In addition, broadcast channels make use of other media for the purposes of programme distribution and communication, such as radio, the printed press, or the Internet – this is called "Off-Air (Design)".

On-Air Promotion: A term used to describe each channel's promotion of its own programmes on air.

Free to Air Programme: A TV programme that is distributed free of charge, and is usually financed by advertising or revenues such as a broadcast license fee.

Live Action: Live shot with a video or film camera.

HDTV / HD: high-definition television. Better quality is achieved through better image resolution.

Distribution Channel: apart from the traditional terrestrial distribution of TV signals, the most common means of distribution are cable and satellite. The market is currently preparing for the switch from analogue to digital signals.

Non-linear TV: in the classic (push) TV world, the flow of the programme determines when you have to watch what, but in a non-linear (pull) TV world, the viewer can choose when he or she wants to view something...

Wipe Effect: a technique mainly used between two programme elements in order to connect them seamlessly by wiping out the following image.

Sundance Film Festival: an independent film festival founded by the actor Robert Redford. http://festival.sundance.org/

PSB: Public Service Broadcasting

IPTV: Internet Protocol Television. Television signals are broadcast over the internet, and can be received by the viewer using an IP set-top box.

(Programme) Packaging: Means the visual design of a specific programme with all of its components, such as an opener, closer, bumper, lower third etc.

2D/3D Animation: Animation uses both two-dimensional and three-dimensional techniques. Nowadays, both types tend to be computer-generated.

16 : 9: The image ratio. The traditional format is 4 : 3, but the higher ratio is used more in film and fills more of the human field of vision.

INDEX

© 2007 daab
cologne london new york

published and distributed worldwide by
daab gmbh
friesenstr. 50
d-50670 köln

p +49 - 221 - 913 927 0
f +49 - 221 - 913 927 20

mail@daab-online.com
www.daab-online.com

publisher ralf daab
rdaab@daab-online.com

creative director feyyaz
mail@feyyaz.com

edited & written by björn bartholdy
bartholdy media project ltd, bergisch gladbach
www.bmpltd.de

book design, layout, imaging & pre-press anja engelke, cologne
www.aenorm.de

english translation catherine grosvenor, edinburgh

dvd opener & sound, eberweinpardeike, cologne
www.ep-studio.de

dvd-authoring, viergrad gmbh, cologne
www.viergrad.de

© about the author photo, dagmar tiboc
page 394

© introduction photos
page 2, 4 PLUG TV / SEVEN
page 396 FUEL TV / signature series #10, dean bradley
page 398 FUEL TV / Ident adapt by shilo

printed in italy
www.printertrento.it

isbn 978-3-86654-025-5